MICROWAVE COOKERY
CORDON BLEU STYLE

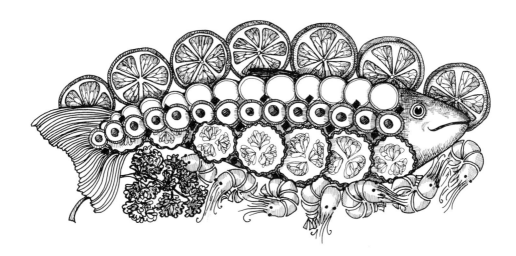

Val Collins

DAVID & CHARLES
Newton Abbot   London   North Pomfret (Vt)

To my husband, Tony, for his support and constant patience, and Pam, for her continued encouragement and guidance.

Acknowledgements

I should also like to express my sincere thanks and gratitude to my colleagues and friends at Thorn EMI Major Domestic Appliances Limited for their support and encouragement and for supplying microwave cookers. Thanks also to Hanningtons of Brighton in assisting with the tableware, and John Jenkins & Sons of Nyewood, Rogate, for supplying the glassware for the frontispiece.

Photography: John Plimmer, RPM Photographic, 10 The Pallant, Havant, Hants

Home economists: Rosemary Moon, Pat Alburey, Clare Hayson and Jane Gregory

Line illustrations: Mona Thorogood

Cover photographs: *front – Paupiettes of Sole Walewska (page 32); back – Hot Strawberries (page 93) and Creamy Rice with Apricots (page 89)* (John Plimmer/RPM Photographic)

The recipes in this book have been developed by Val Collins and not by The Cordon Bleu Cookery School.

British Library Cataloguing in Publication Data

Collins, Val
    Microwave Cookery Cordon Bleu Style.
    1. Microwave cookery
    I. Title
    641.5'882   TX832

    ISBN 0-7153-8781-2

Phototypeset by ABM Typographics Limited, Hull
and printed in The Netherlands
by Smeets Offset BV, Weert
for David & Charles Publishers plc
Brunel House   Newton Abbot   Devon

Published in the United States of America
by David & Charles Inc
North Pomfret   Vermont 05053   USA

Contents

Foreword

Louis XV of France was a great gourmet and his reign saw many developments in the culinary art. The very term cordon bleu was strictly applied to woman cooks only and originated from an enthusiastic recognition of female merit by the king himself. The award was given by the French government during the seventeenth and eighteenth centuries to skilful female cooks who passed an examination in culinary distinction and was in the form of a medal suspended on a dark blue ribbon. Cordon bleu today is based on French cooking methods and does not necessarily mean *haute cuisine* although the two are very often considered synonymous – the humble steak and kidney pie can be cordon bleu if it is well cooked and presented in style.

Cooking is an art, beloved by those who enjoy to eat good food and cherished by those who enjoy producing it. But you don't have to be a genius to cook. Start off slowly as you would any other branch of learning and you can attain great heights. Don't hesitate there though, as continued patience, willingness and carefulness will ensure a constant high standard to astound your friends and delight yourself. Most of all, good cooking is about inventiveness and adaptation to new ideas and skills, and the experienced microwave cook will applaud the chance to exploit the microwave cooker to the full and explore its use in producing exciting cordon bleu meals. There will be the sceptics who question how microwave cookers and good food can possibly go together, and doubters who worry about possible negative effects on favourite dishes. 'I prefer traditional methods' they often say, yet I know hardly one who would prefer to throw out the modern conventional cooker and cook Sunday lunch over an open fire in the hearth to produce the real traditional roast!

Just as any other modern kitchen appliance has taken the chore out of kitchen management, so the microwave cooker can offer a convenience to today's lifestyle, while at the same time producing better, tastier food. With its speed of cooking and the fact that very little additional liquid or fat is required, foods take on a fresher, brighter appearance and add a new natural dimension to our daily meal. Gone are the days of discoloured and uninteresting vegetables which did absolutely nothing to please the eye, let alone the palate. Fish too can be cooked in their own juices – not needing vast amounts of court bouillon – to achieve a wonderful moist result. And just think of the saving on nutrients which are normally thrown away with the cooking liquid. Thank goodness the microwave cooker is no longer looked on as just a 'defroster' or 'reheater', although it certainly does those jobs well and efficiently. But think of it as a versatile tool and general factotum, for it will boil, poach, steam, melt, soften, simmer, keep warm as well as bake and roast to produce delicious succulent results.

The sales of microwave cookers have escalated over the past few years and are continuing to increase with a huge variety of worktop and built-in models available to suit all. Manufacturers and retailers are now well into the replacement market as the original models with basic on/off controls are being changed for cookers with more sophisticated features, including microwave combined with conventional ovens.

So don't be left behind, set in your culinary ways. Let your microwave cooker help you to produce the tried and tested recipes I have prepared for you here and create exciting meals to please the most discerning of cooks and fit to set before a king!

Introduction

Successful results from the microwave cooker are dependent upon a few special considerations regarding its use. It is important to understand all the facts given in the manufacturer's user instructions and the recommendations on procedures should always be followed.

For this book of cordon bleu recipes, I have assumed that the reader has already taken the first steps into the world of microwave cookery – perhaps with a reputable book on the subject – and is familiar with the basic terminology and cooking techniques.

Power levels and timings

I have referred to the various power levels required for the recipes as percentages of 'full' or 'high' power (100%), as microwave cookers have yet to be standardised and descriptions of settings vary considerably. Remember to check the percentage power levels and the description of the settings for your own model.

The recipes in this book were divised and tested in microwave cookers with power outputs of 650 watts. Your own model may have a higher or lower output and therefore cooking times must be adjusted to account for this. The following is a comparison and guide to timings on 100% (full) setting in ovens of different outputs.

600–700W	500–600W	400–500W
30 sec	35 sec	40 sec
1 min	1 min 10 sec	1 min 20 sec
5 min	5 min 45 sec	6 min 45 sec
10 min	11 min 30 sec	13 min 30 sec
20 min	23 min	27 min
30 min	34 min 30 sec	40 min 30 sec
1 hr	1 hr 10 min	1 hr 20 min

Success with recipes

The important thing in microwave cooking is to master the principles first and then allow the application of the rules for special dishes to follow as a matter of course. As experience is gained, so confidence will grow. Remember it is not necessary to serve highly complicated dishes when you entertain. Some of the most mouthwatering results come from good, plain dishes like the traditional country casseroles of the French regional cuisine. Easily adapted for the microwave cook, they can be prepared in advance ready for reheating when required, leaving ample time for relaxing and enjoying pre-dinner drinks with guests.

The fundamental necessities for good cooking are quality and freshness – the best butter and olive oil; shallots, onions and garlic; rich stocks and quality wines for cooking; coarse salt and freshly ground black pepper; the best wine vinegar and a selection of fresh herbs and spices as well as prime-choice basic foods.

The ingredients

Fats
When cooking in the microwave, the amount of fats for use in recipes can be reduced considerably if required, due to the moist cooking conditions. In my view, of all the fats, nothing quite replaces the flavour of butter in cooking. Unsalted butter has a delicious creamy taste and it is always easier to add salt than take it away. Butter should be used from room temperature when cook-

ing in the microwave, particularly when softening or melting, otherwise it may splutter.

Fat pork and bacon give a deep richness and flavour essential for country casseroles while lard, dripping and poultry fats are required for regional variations.

Of the vegetable oils, olive and corn oils are practical and pleasant to use. A good olive oil is a must for salads and sauces for pasta. The more expensive nut oils, such as walnut and hazelnut, are distinctive in flavour and can be used with butter or to blend with a mild-flavoured seed oil, such as sunflower or grapeseed.

Although clarified butter is often suggested and can be used as an alternative to ghee, it does not have the distinctive flavour required for some recipes.

Pears in Tarragon Cream (page 12)

Herbs, spices, aromatics and seasonings
The clever use of these will impart the most delicious flavours to your microwave cooking and help to make food just a little more special. Don't omit them from the recipes or use substitutes or the authentic flavours will be lost. Use them with care though, as the speed of microwave cooking tends to accentuate flavours and delicate foods in particular can be easily masked by their over-use. Wherever possible, use fresh herbs as they give the best flavours. Otherwise, use herbs which have been dried in the microwave for excellent colours and retained flavours (page 10).

Salt *can* be used but as a general rule microwave-cooked food requires much less of it. Use minimal amounts and dissolve it in a liquid ingredient rather than sprinkle directly onto the food.

Stocks
Home-made stocks from carcasses, bones, vegetables and herbs are a must for good cooking. They give essential flavours to soups and casseroles and the right consistency for good sauces. Small amounts at a time can be quickly made in the microwave when you have the ingredients available, and then frozen in smaller quantities to provide a continuous supply for your cooking.

Cut down the amount added to dishes if thickening relies on the reduction of liquids during cooking.

Wines
A small selection of alcoholic drinks, including wines, liqueur miniatures and small bottles of kitchen vermouth, sherry and brandy, provides a basic kitchen storecupboard or 'bar' – for the food, not the cook! Wine in particular is an ideal standby to add a special something to the most basic of foods.

Cream and yoghurt
Cream in all its forms is a luxurious complement associated with sumptious foods and adds a subtlety in richness, flavour and texture to both sweet and savoury dishes.

Of all the natural plain yoghurts available, the low-fat varieties provide a lightness in texture, but the thick strained Greek yoghurt has the best flavour and gives a creamier effect to dishes. Heat with care in the microwave and check frequently to prevent overcooking and separation.

The basic foods

Meat
For best results, a joint should be regular in shape so that it will have a better appearance and cook evenly – rolled joints or top leg of lamb or pork are ideal. Projecting knuckles and bones from shoulder and leg joints or crown roasts should be shielded with small, smooth pieces of aluminium foil for half the cooking time.

Cooking in the microwave will not always tenderise meat in the same way as cooking conventionally, so prime cuts give best results together with the

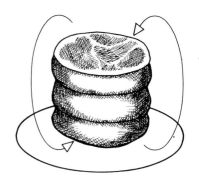

Joints should be turned over half way through the cooking time

Protect the breast and ends of drumsticks with foil

choice of the correct power setting. Marinate cheaper cuts to help tenderise them before cooking.

When 'roasting' joints, use a 50–80% power setting, and when casseroling or stewing, a 30–50% setting, depending on the type of meat.

Poultry

Truss whole birds well before cooking to ensure a neat, compact shape. Protect vulnerable areas with foil, including the breast of larger birds, although this may not be necessary if it is cooked breast side down for the first half of the cooking time.

Game

Game birds and venison which are young and tender are suitable for cooking in the same way as poultry and joints. Meat from older, tougher birds and animals should be marinated before cooking and is better suited to simmering at a 30% setting.

Offal

Popping of foods such as kidney and liver can happen during cooking and is caused by heat build-up inside small vessels or membranes which eventually burst. Ensure skin and piping and cores of kidneys are removed and turn to a lower power setting should popping occur. Offal cooks well in the microwave providing, as in conventional cooking, the power level (or heat setting) is chosen to suit the type being cooked.

Eggs and cheese

These are both high-protein foods and as such are sensitive to heat – both will become leathery in texture if overcooked. Yolks set before the whites, due to the high-fat and protein content which absorbs microwaves more readily, and cheese melts quickly. Allow a little less time at first and cook for a few seconds longer if necessary. Egg yolks should always be pricked with a sharp pointed knife or cocktail stick, or steam build-up inside the membrane will cause it to explode.

Reduce power settings when necessary for egg sauces and egg-based dishes, or check frequently and stir to ensure even cooking. Standing times are also important (except for omelettes and soufflé-type dishes), and dishes are best removed from the oven when barely set and allowed to finish cooking during the standing time.

If a brown topping is required for cheese and au gratin dishes, place them under a hot conventional grill for a few minutes before serving.

Arrange fish head to tail in a single layer; when cooking whole fish, rearrange them half way through cooking and shield vulnerable areas with foil

Fish and shellfish

Fish is particularly excellent when cooked in the microwave. Clean and prepare in the normal way, ensuring that whole fish are gutted, thoroughly cleaned and washed. Slit the skin of whole fish at the thickest part to allow steam to escape and pierce the membranes of fish eyes before cooking.

The arrangement of fish when cooking several together is important. Place in a single layer, head to tail and overlapping slightly to protect the thinner parts from overcooking. Alternatively, tuck the thinner parts of fillets under to achieve an even depth, or roll up. Cutlets and steaks should be arranged with the thicker parts towards the outside of the dish. Test at regular intervals; when done the flesh will flake easily and have a slightly opaque appearance. If it is still translucent, it may be left to stand or cooked for a little longer.

Shellfish should be cooked using the guidelines for fish above. Live shellfish should be killed by conventional methods.

Most cooking can be carried out at 100% (full), although larger whole fish and thicker steaks or middle cuts of salmon or cod will benefit from a lower 30–50% setting.

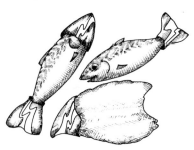

Rice, pasta and pulses

They cook extremely well in the microwave but there's not much time saving. The main advantage is that little or no attention is required during cooking and the kitchen remains relatively free of steam. Ensure the container is large enough to allow for the water to boil and the expansion of the food.

Always add boiling water from the kettle, and a little salt may be added to rice and pasta, but not to pulses as it prevents them from softening, therefore extending the cooking time. A spoonful of oil added to pasta will prevent sticking; push down any pieces protruding above the water level until softened before placing in the microwave to cook.

Cover and cook at 100% (full) setting for white rice and pasta. After soaking, pulses should be covered and boiled initially on 100% (full) for 10–12 minutes and then reduced to 50% setting for the remaining time. Brown and wild rice also require a 50% setting to cook through after initial boiling.

Fruit and vegetables

Choose seasonal varieties in peak condition and of similar size. When appropriate, cut or slice into uniform sizes to ensure even cooking. Minimal liquid is required, and for vegetables remember to add salt to the liquid to prevent toughening during cooking. Stir once or twice and watch the timings. For crisp results, undercook rather than overcook as vegetables will continue to cook by residual heat during any standing period.

Fruits and vegetables to be cooked whole – jacket potatoes, aubergines, tomatoes and apples for example – should be pricked or scored to prevent bursting, and preferably larger ones should be turned over halfway through cooking.

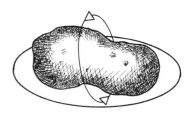

When cooking foods of uneven shape such as broccoli spears, place the tender parts towards the centre of the dish; larger jacket potatoes should be turned over halfway through cooking

Cook's hints and tips

Barbecue

Meat or poultry can be part-cooked in the microwave before placing on the barbecue to help prevent it from charring on the outside while trying to get the centre cooked through.

Blanching

Small quantities of vegetables can be blanched before freezing by cooking for about half their recommended cooking time. In addition, peeled potatoes may be blanched prior to roasting or frying conventionally.

Breadcrumbs

To dry breadcrumbs, spread about 50g (2oz) fresh crumbs on a double thickness of absorbent kitchen paper and heat in the microwave for about 2 min. Check every minute and toss them over if necessary. To toast them in butter, stir the fresh crumbs in 25g (1oz) melted butter in a shallow dish or plate. Cook them, uncovered, for 3–4 min, checking and stirring every minute.

Bread rolls

Warm rolls in a wicker basket lined with a napkin or paper serviette before serving at lunch or dinner. Heat 6 rolls for ¾–1 min or 12 for 1½–2 min, depending on the type of bread. Leave for about 1 min before serving.

Cheese

Ripen cream cheese such as brie when in a hurry by giving about 30 sec at a time on 30% setting, until soft, but remove it as soon as it is warm or beginning to melt.

Bread rolls can be warmed ready to serve in a lined wicker basket

Chocolate

Melt chocolate quickly and easily without fuss. Break into pieces and heat for 1½ min at a time until softened enough to stir and blend.

Citrus fruits
Oranges, lemons, grapefruits and limes will yield more juice if warmed in the microwave for a few seconds until just hot, before squeezing.

Coffee
Make extra filtered coffee in advance for lunch or dinner parties and reheat it as required in suitable microwave jugs.

Coffee beans
Refresh stale coffee beans in the microwave on a plate or in a shallow dish by warming until just hot, stirring once.

Dried fruits
Speed up the soaking process by heating in the microwave with just enough water to cover. Cover the dish and heat until boiling and cook for 2 min. Leave for up to 1 hr to swell and soften.

Herbs
Dry your own herbs in the microwave for best flavours and aromas. Place about 25g (1oz) between layers of absorbent kitchen paper and heat for a minute at a time until dry and brittle. Turn once or twice throughout.

Jams, syrups and honey
Remove the cap from the glass jar or place a quantity into a bowl. Heat for 15 sec at a time until just warm. This will make spreading and measuring by the spoonful much easier.

Lemon zest
To dry, spread finely grated rind between absorbent kitchen paper and heat for 30 sec at a time until dry and crumbly. Leave to cool before storing.

Sauces and gravies
Make them in advance and place in their serving jugs to be quickly reheated when required; 275ml (½pt) sauce will take 2–3 min. Stir well before serving.

Spirits and liqueurs
For flambé dishes, hot toddies and liqueur coffees, pour 2–4 × 15ml tbsp (2–4tbsp) into a glass and heat for 10–20 sec.

Sugar and salt
To soften hard or damp sugar or salt, heat in the microwave for 30–60 sec.

Toasted almonds
Toast nuts, desiccated coconut and sesame seeds, without needing to add oil or fat, by heating in the microwave (use an uncovered heatproof plate or shallow dish) for 4–6 min depending on quantity. Toss them once or twice.

Tomatoes and peaches
To remove the skin, first slit it then heat in the microwave for 30–60 sec until just hot. Leave to stand for a minute before peeling. If skinning a quantity of fruit, the traditional boiling-water method will be easier.

Yeast doughs
Warm the flour and liquid ingredients for bread-making to ensure the mixture is at an even temperature throughout to help the proving process. To prove in the microwave, warm the dough, covered, for 15 sec at a time and allow 5–15 min rest, depending on the type of dough; repeat until risen.

Gigot of Lamb with Redcurrant Glaze (page 37); Calabrese with Poulette Sauce (page 69); Pâté de Fois Gras with Quail Eggs (page 12)

Hors d'oeuvres and salads

Pears in tarragon cream (serves 6)   colour page 6
POWER LEVEL: 60%

6 dessert pears, evenly sized and preferably with their stalks
few drops lemon juice
275ml (½pt) double cream
2 × 15ml tbsp (2tbsp) tarragon vinegar
caster sugar
salt and freshly ground black pepper
for garnish: tarragon leaves

1 Peel the pears and core them from the base, leaving the stalks intact. Cut a small slice from the bottom of each pear and stand them in a dish.
2 Brush or sprinkle them with a few drops of lemon juice. Cover and cook for 10–12 min until just tender, rearranging the pears halfway through cooking if necessary. Leave to cool.
3 Beat the cream and vinegar together until thick and season to taste with caster sugar, salt and freshly ground black pepper.
4 Drain the pears and arrange them on individual serving plates. Coat them with the tarragon cream and garnish with tarragon leaves. Serve immediately.

DO NOT FREEZE

Pâté de foie gras with quail eggs (serves 6)   colour page 11
POWER LEVEL: 100% (FULL)

6 quail eggs
225g (8oz) pâté de foie gras
24 stoneless black or green olives
300g (10oz) can beef consommé
2 × 5ml tsp (2tsp) gelatin
for garnish: chopped parsley

1 Cook the quail eggs conventionally in a pan of boiling water for 4 min. Drain the eggs and plunge them into a bowl of cold water. Shell the eggs and leave them in a bowl of cold water.
2 Divide the pâté into 6 and spread each piece over the base and sides of 6 individual small dishes or ramekins. Nest a cold quail egg into each one and surround it with 4 olives.
3 Place 3 × 15ml tbsp (3tbsp) of the consommé into a small bowl and sprinkle on the gelatin. Stir lightly and heat in the microwave for 15–30 sec until the gelatin has softened. Stir until completely dissolved.
4 Add the rest of the consommé to the gelatin and spoon it over the pâté and quail eggs. Place in the refrigerator for about 1 hr until set.
5 Garnish each one with chopped parsley before serving cold.

DO NOT FREEZE

Cook's note: If pâté de fois gras is difficult to find, this easy recipe works just as well with another smooth-textured pâté of your choice

Chicken livers with vermouth (serves 6)
POWER LEVEL: 100% (FULL)

40g (1½oz) butter
6 lean bacon rashers, derinded and cut into strips
675g (1½lb) chicken livers, cut into halves
salt and freshly ground black pepper
3–4 × 15ml tbsp (3–4tbsp) red vermouth
1 × 15ml tbsp (1tbsp) chopped fresh sage
kneaded butter made with 25g (1oz) softened butter and 20g (¾oz) flour
for serving: spinach or chard and vinaigrette dressing (page 78)

1 Melt the butter in a casserole dish or bowl for 1–1½ min, add the bacon and cook, covered, for 4 min, stirring once halfway through cooking.
2 Stir in the chicken livers and continue to cook for a further 8–10 min, mixing well twice throughout.
3 Add seasoning to taste, the vermouth and sage and cook for a further 1 min. Stir in the kneaded butter a little at a time and cook, uncovered, until thickened, stirring every minute.
4 Remove the thicker stalks of the spinach or chard leaves. Wash the leaves well and shake dry. Toss in a vinaigrette dressing and serve on a platter.
5 Serve the chicken livers warm on the bed of spinach or chard.

Cook's note: Try this recipe replacing the red vermouth and sage with white wine and some peeled, halved and deseeded green grapes. It makes a delicious starter served with fingers of toast, or a supper dish served on hot buttered toast

Salade tiède (*serves 6*)

POWER LEVEL: 100% (FULL)

This salad is served warm and includes chicory, walnuts, bacon and duck livers

1 Place the walnut oil into a bowl and heat for 1½ min. Add the bacon and cook, uncovered, for 5–6 min until slightly crisp, stirring once throughout.
2 Cut each duck liver into 6 pieces, and add to the bacon with the garlic and continue to cook for a further 1½–2 min stirring halfway through cooking. Add the walnuts and cook for 30 sec.
3 Rinse a suitable microwave salad bowl or dish in water, shake off most of the water and place the bowl in the microwave for 30–45 sec to warm through.
4 Dry the bowl and toss in the chicory and watercress. Lift the bacon, liver and walnut mixture with a draining spoon onto the salad vegetables.
5 Add the cider vinegar to the cooking dish and stir to mix any residue. Cook for 30 sec and then pour over the salad.
6 Quickly add seasoning to taste, toss over lightly and serve immediately.

DO NOT FREEZE

2–3 × 15ml tbsp (2–3tbsp) walnut oil
6 rashers smoked streaky bacon, derinded and cut into strips
4 duck livers
1 clove garlic, crushed
40–50g (1½–2oz) walnuts, coarsely chopped
3 chicory heads, trimmed and sliced diagonally
½ bunch watercress, thick stems removed
2 × 15ml tbsp (2tbsp) cider vinegar
salt and freshly ground black pepper

Artichokes with vinaigrette (*serves 4*)

POWER LEVEL: 100% (FULL)

1 Trim off the stalks from the bottom of the artichokes and cut away any marked or discoloured points of the leaves with scissors. Place the artichokes into a large dish with the salted water, cover and cook for 15–20 min, turning the dish or rearranging the artichokes halfway through if necessary. Drain, refresh in cold water and leave to cool.
2 Place 2 × 15ml tbsp (2tbsp) of the oil into a bowl or dish with the shallots or onions. Mix well, cover and cook for 3 min. Stir in the mushrooms and continue to cook for a further 2 min. Leave to cool.
3 Add the wine, wine vinegar and the remaining oil. Season to taste with salt and pepper and finally stir in the garlic and ham. Allow the mixture to marinate for 15 min.
4 Pull out some of the centre leaves from each artichoke to reveal the choke and remove this by scraping carefully with a spoon. Put a spoonful of the dressing in the centre of each artichoke.
5 Serve on individual plates sprinkled with the herbs and the rest of the dressing handed separately.

DO NOT FREEZE

4 medium globe artichokes
150ml (¼pt) salted water
6 × 15ml tbsp (6tbsp) olive oil
2 shallots or small onions, finely chopped
50g (2oz) mushrooms, finely chopped
3 × 15ml tbsp (3tbsp) dry white wine
2 × 15ml tbsp (2tbsp) white wine vinegar
salt and freshly ground black pepper
1 clove garlic, crushed
75g (3oz) ham, finely chopped
1 × 15ml tbsp (1tbsp) chopped fresh mixed herbs

Duck with Herbs (page 52) and
Almond Croquettes (page 70);
Mussels with Saffron Rice and
Walnut and Garlic Dressing (below)

25g (1oz) butter
2 cloves garlic, crushed
4 rashers lean back bacon
8 × 15ml tbsp (8tbsp) browned
  breadcrumbs
salt and freshly ground black
  pepper
12 oysters in their half shells
3–4 × 15ml tbsp (3–4tbsp)
  grated parmesan cheese
slivers butter
for garnish: chopped parsley

30 mussels approximately,
  cleaned and scraped
3 × 15ml tbsp (3tbsp) dry white
  wine
4 × 15ml tbsp (4tbsp) fish stock
  (page 21)
1 shallot or small onion, finely
  chopped

for the rice stuffing:
100g (4oz) long-grain rice
2 × 15ml tbsp (2tbsp) olive oil
1 large onion, finely chopped
50g (2oz) pine nuts or walnuts,
  coarsely chopped
25g (1oz) currants
1–2 × 5ml tsp (1–2tsp) sugar to
  taste
salt and freshly ground black
  pepper
1 × 15ml tbsp (1tbsp) chopped
  parsley
550ml (1pt) fish stock (page 21),
  approximately
pinch saffron

for the walnut and garlic dressing:
2 slices bread, crusts removed
water
2–3 cloves garlic, roughly
  chopped
100g (4oz) walnuts
salt and freshly ground black
  pepper
1 × 15ml tbsp (1tbsp) olive oil
2 × 15ml tbsp (2tbsp) wine
  vinegar or lemon juice

Huitres gratinées *(serves 4)*
POWER LEVEL: 100% (FULL)

1 Melt the butter in a bowl for 1 min, add the garlic, cover and cook for 1 min.
2 Remove the rind from the bacon and cut the rashers into thin strips. Place onto a plate and cover lightly with kitchen paper towel. Cook for 4–5 min until the pieces of bacon are crispy, tossing them over halfway through. Drain on kitchen paper towel.
3 Add the browned breadcrumbs to the butter and garlic, toss well in the butter and season lightly with salt and freshly ground black pepper.
4 Drain the excess liquid from the oysters. Spoon over the breadcrumb mixture. Scatter with the bacon, sprinkle on the parmesan cheese and top with slivers of butter.
5 Arrange half the oysters on a large plate or on the microwave cooker shelf and cook, uncovered, for 2–3 min, rearranging the shells halfway through if necessary. Keep warm while cooking the rest of the oysters.
6 Serve straight away sprinkled with a little chopped parsley.

DO NOT FREEZE

Mussels with saffron rice and walnut and garlic dressing
(serves 4–6)   *colour opposite*
POWER LEVEL: 100% (FULL) AND 50%

1 Place the mussels into a large bowl or dish with the wine, fish stock and shallot or onion. Cover and cook for 5–6 min until the shells have opened, stirring or shaking the dish 2–3 times throughout.
2 Drain off the liquid from the mussels and reserve. Leave the mussels to cool, remove them from the dish and discard the surplus half shells and any mussels which have not opened during cooking.
3 If necessary, wash the rice for the stuffing and drain well. Place the olive oil and onion in the bowl or dish, mix well together, cover and cook for 3 min.
4 Add the rice, pine nuts or walnuts, currants, sugar and seasoning to taste, parsley, half the fish stock, saffron and the reserved liquid from the mussels. Stir well together.
5 Cover and cook for 10 min on 100% (full) then reduce to 50% setting and continue to cook until the liquid has been absorbed and the rice is tender. Stir the mixture occasionally during cooking and add more stock as necessary. Remove the cover from the dish for the last 1–2 min to dry out the rice and then leave to cool.
6 For the dressing, soak the bread slices in a little water and then squeeze dry. Place the garlic and walnuts into a blender or food processor and chop finely. Add the bread, seasoning, oil and vinegar or lemon juice and process until thick.
7 Pile teaspoonfuls of the rice stuffing into each mussel and arrange attractively on a serving platter or dish. Serve cold with the dressing handed separately.

DO NOT FREEZE

Cook's note: *Before cooking the mussels, check that they are all closed. Any which are open should be tapped sharply on the shell with a spoon. If they do not contract and close, they should be discarded*

225g (8oz) ripe tomatoes,
skinned, deseeded and
chopped *or* 1 × 400g (14oz)
can tomatoes, drained and
sieved
1 × 5ml tsp (1tsp) salt
¼ × 5ml tsp (¼tsp) ground
black pepper
1 × 15ml tbsp (1tbsp) lemon
juice
100ml (4fl oz) olive oil
8 thin slices cooked chicken
breast
for garnish: small bunch
watercress

Chicken with tomato vinaigrette *(serves 4)* *colour page 59*
POWER LEVEL: 100% (FULL)

1 Place the tomatoes into a bowl or dish and cook, uncovered, for 7–9 min until reduced to a thick pulp, stirring once or twice throughout. Leave to cool.
2 Place the salt, pepper, lemon juice and oil into a blender or food processor and blend together. Alternatively place the ingredients into a small screw-top jar and shake vigorously until blended.
3 Combine the cooled tomato purée with the vinaigrette and add extra seasoning to taste if necessary.
4 Pour the tomato vinaigrette onto a serving platter and arrange the chicken slices in a circle on the top. Garnish the centre of the dish with a neat bunch of watercress and serve.

DO NOT FREEZE

Cook's note: *Any cold meat or vegetables could be used instead of the chicken*

175g (6oz) dried chestnuts
boiling water
275ml (½pt) boiling vegetable
stock (page 20)
1 shallot or small onion
225g (8oz) cooked duck meat
150ml (¼pt) double cream
2 × 15ml tbsp (2tbsp)
mayonnaise (page 76)
½ × 5ml tsp (½tsp) grated
nutmeg
salt and freshly ground black
pepper
150ml (¼pt) dry white wine or
stock
1 envelope gelatin
for garnish: watercress
for serving: thinly sliced toast

Duck and chestnut mousse *(serves 8)*
POWER LEVEL: 100% (FULL) AND 50%

1 Cover the chestnuts with boiling water in a bowl, cover with a lid or pierced clingfilm and cook for 5 min. Leave to stand for 1 hr to swell.
2 Drain the chestnuts, add the boiling stock, cover again and cook for 10 min on 100% (full) then a further 10–15 min on 50% setting. Purée the chestnuts with the stock in a blender or food processor.
3 Finely chop the shallot or onion and the duck meat in the blender or food processor or put through a mincer. Add the chestnuts, cream, mayonnaise, nutmeg and seasoning and mix well together.
4 Heat the wine or stock for 2 min, add the gelatin and stir well. Heat for a further 15–30 sec until completely dissolved, if necessary. Stir the gelatin into the mousse.
5 Rinse a 17·5cm (7in) ring mould in cold water. Fill with the mousse, smooth the surface and chill until firm. Turn out onto a serving dish or plate and garnish with watercress. Serve with thinly sliced toast.

225g (8oz) wild rice
500ml (18fl oz) boiling water
3 × 15ml tbsp (3tbsp) oil
225g (8oz) mushrooms,
coarsely chopped
1 × 15ml tbsp (1tbsp) lemon
juice
2 hard-boiled eggs, coarsely
chopped
1 green pepper, deseeded and
finely chopped
200g (7oz) peeled shrimps (or
prawns)
salt and freshly ground black
pepper
25–50g (1–2oz) pistachios,
shelled
for garnish: tomato slices
for serving: aïoli sauce
(page 76)

Wild rice, mushroom and shrimp salad with aïoli *(serves 4–6)*
POWER LEVEL: 100% (FULL) AND 30% *colour page 55*

1 Wash the rice thoroughly and drain well. Place the rice into a bowl or dish and stir in the boiling water.
2 Cover and cook for 5 min on 100% (full) and a further 40–50 min on 30% setting until the rice is tender, stirring occasionally during cooking. Leave to cool.
3 Place the oil in a bowl or dish with the mushrooms and lemon juice and cook, uncovered, for about 3 min until the mushrooms are tender, stirring once halfway through cooking. Leave to cool.
4 Add the mushrooms, eggs, pepper and shrimps (or prawns) to the rice and place into a salad bowl. Add seasoning to taste and fork over lightly. Sprinkle with the pistachios and garnish with tomato slices. Serve cold with the aïoli sauce.

DO NOT FREEZE

Cook's note: *Wild rice can be difficult to obtain in some areas so busmati or brown rice make good substitutes*

Turkey and avocado salad with roquefort dressing *(serves 4–6)*
POWER LEVEL: 100% (FULL)   *colour page 27*

1   Place the turkey breast fillet onto a plate and sprinkle with a few drops of lemon juice, a little black pepper and brush with the oil.
2   Cover the plate with a plate cover or pierced clingfilm and cook for 4½–5½ min, turning the turkey over halfway through cooking. Leave covered and allow to cool.
3   Peel, halve and stone the avocado and cut into thin slices. Sprinkle the slices with the rest of the lemon juice.
4   Wash and dry the watercress and cut the celery heart into thin slices. Quarter the hard-boiled eggs and thinly slice the tomatoes.
5   Place all the ingredients for the dressing into a blender or food processor and blend until smooth.
6   When the turkey has cooled, cut the fillet into thin strips or slices.
7   Either arrange the ingredients for the salad attractively on a large platter or toss them gently together and place in a salad bowl.
8   Pour over the roquefort dressing and serve.

DO NOT FREEZE

350g (12oz) turkey breast fillet
½ lemon, juice
freshly ground black pepper
1 × 15ml tbsp (1tbsp) oil
1 ripe avocado pear
1 bunch watercress
1 celery heart
2 hard-boiled eggs
2 tomatoes

for the roquefort dressing:
40g (1½oz) roquefort cheese
salt and pepper
3 × 15ml tbsp (3tbsp) wine vinegar
5–6 × 15ml tbsp (5–6tbsp) olive oil

Potato salad with parma ham *(serves 4–6)*   *colour page 59*
POWER LEVEL: 100% (FULL)

1   Place the potatoes into a large bowl or dish with the salted water. Cover and cook for 10–15 min until tender, stirring twice during cooking.
2   Drain the potatoes and peel away the skins. Cut the potatoes into thick slices and keep warm.
3   Rub the inside of a salad bowl or dish with the half cloves of garlic. Put the potatoes into the bowl with the onion, gherkins, capers, parsley, chives and tarragon. Season with salt and freshly ground black pepper and add the parma ham.
4   Cut the hard-boiled eggs into halves. Remove the yolks and place into a blender or food processor with the vinegar, oils and salt and pepper to taste. Process until well blended.
5   Pour the dressing over the salad and mix well. Serve warm with the egg whites chopped and sprinkled over the top.

DO NOT FREEZE

450–675g (1–1½lb) new potatoes, scrubbed
4–6 × 15ml tbsp (4–6tbsp) salted water
1 clove garlic, cut in half
1 onion, sliced
2 × 15ml tbsp (2tbsp) chopped gherkins
1 × 15ml tbsp (1tbsp) chopped capers
1 × 15ml tbsp (1tbsp) chopped parsley
2 × 5ml tsp (2tsp) finely chopped chives
1 × 5ml tsp (1tsp) finely chopped tarragon
salt and freshly ground black pepper
75g (3oz) parma ham, cut into thin strips
2 hard-boiled eggs
3 × 15ml tbsp (3tbsp) vinegar
4 × 15ml tbsp (4tbsp) walnut oil
100ml (4fl oz) peanut oil

Prawns baked in soured cream *(serves 6)*
POWER LEVEL: 70%

1   Lightly butter 6 ovenproof small dishes or ramekins. Spoon the prawns into the dishes and sprinkle with freshly ground black pepper.
2   Pour over the soured cream and cover with a thin layer of breadcrumbs. Top with slivers of butter and cook, uncovered, for 10 min.
3   Brown the tops under a hot grill and serve straight away, garnished with sprigs of parsley.

DO NOT FREEZE

350g (12oz) peeled prawns
black pepper
215ml (7½fl oz) soured cream
3–4 × 15ml tbsp (3–4tbsp) fine, fresh brown breadcrumbs
slivers butter
for garnish: sprigs parsley

550ml (1pt) mussels, cleaned
  and scraped
1 shallot, finely chopped
1 clove garlic, crushed
1 bay leaf
150ml (¼pt) dry white wine
175g (6oz) sole or plaice fillet,
  skinned
175g (6oz) sea bass or halibut,
  filleted and skinned
4 scallops
50g (2oz) peeled prawns
50g (2oz) crab meat
275ml (½pt) velouté sauce
  (page 76 and method 5)
salt and freshly ground black
  pepper
2 × 15ml tbsp (2tbsp) chopped
  parsley or dill
4 × 10cm (4in) baked vol-au-
  vent cases with lids
for garnish: 4 unpeeled prawns
  and sprigs of parsley

Seafood vol-au-vents (serves 4)   colour opposite
POWER LEVEL: 100% (FULL)

1   Place the mussels, shallot, garlic, bay leaf and 3 × 15ml tbsp (3tbsp) of
    the wine into a large bowl or dish. Cover with a lid or pierced clingfilm and
    cook for 4–5 min until the shells are open, tossing well halfway through.
2   Allow to stand for a few minutes to cool, then remove the mussels from
    their shells. Discard the shells and reserve the cooking liquid.
3   Cut the sole or plaice fillet and the sea bass or halibut into small pieces.
    Cut each scallop into quarters and place into a bowl or dish with the fish.
    Add the remaining wine, cover and cook for 3 min.
4   Stir in the prawns and crab meat and continue to cook for a further 2 min.
    Drain off and reserve the cooking liquid and keep the fish warm.
5   Using the reserved liquids from the mussels and fish, make up to 275ml
    (½pt) with fish stock or water to prepare the velouté sauce (page 76).
6   Stir the fish into the sauce. Adjust the seasoning to taste and stir in the
    parsley or dill. Spoon the filling into the vol-au-vent cases. Top with the
    lids and garnish each one with an unpeeled prawn (heads removed if
    preferred) and a sprig of parsley. Serve immediately.

DO NOT FREEZE

Cook's note: *A good variety of seafood for the sauce is the secret to produce a
wonderful flavour. When time permits, make your own vol-au-vent cases, otherwise there are some most acceptable ones to buy from good bakeries*

2 × 15ml tbsp (2tbsp) grated
  parmesan cheese
50g (2oz) butter
50g (2oz) flour
225ml (8fl oz) milk
450g (1lb) spinach (or sorrel),
  washed and thicker stalks
  removed
50g (2oz) parmesan cheese,
  finely grated
1 × 15ml tbsp (1tbsp) chopped
  parsley
4 eggs, separated
salt and freshly ground black
  pepper
for serving: hollandaise sauce
  (page 77 and method 6)

Spinach soufflé with hollandaise sauce (serves 4–6)
POWER LEVEL: 100% (FULL)
CONVENTIONAL OVEN TEMPERATURE: 200°C (400°F) MARK 6

Sorrel can replace the spinach as an alternative

1   Lightly butter a 1 litre (1¾pt) soufflé dish. Sprinkle the 2 × 15ml tbsp
    (2tbsp) grated parmesan cheese into the dish and roll it around to coat
    the base and side of the dish.
2   Melt the 50g (2oz) butter in a bowl or dish for 1–1½ min in the microwave,
    stir in the flour and blend well together. Add the milk gradually, return
    the sauce to the microwave and cook for 3–4 min, uncovered, until
    thickened and boiling, stirring every 30 sec. Leave to cool.
3   Place the spinach or sorrel into a covered bowl with just the water clinging
    to the leaves and cook for 6–8 min, stirring well 2–3 times throughout.
    Drain thoroughly in a fine sieve and roughly chop with a spoon to break
    up the leaves.
4   Add the spinach or sorrel to the sauce with the parmesan cheese, parsley
    and egg yolks, beating well together. Add seasoning to taste.
5   Whisk the egg whites until stiff and combine with the sauce, folding and
    cutting with a metal spoon or spatula in a figure of eight movement
    until blended.
6   Turn the mixture into the prepared dish and bake in a preheated oven
    for 30–40 min until risen and golden brown. While the soufflé is cooking,
    make the hollandaise sauce.
7   Serve the soufflé immediately accompanied by the hollandaise sauce.

DO NOT FREEZE

*Seafood Vol-au-vents (above);
Goose Ballotine (page 49)*

Soups and stocks

Stocks

Stocks, made from bones and a few vegetables, form the simple basis of home-made soups providing a source of natural goodness and excellent flavour. Small quantities of stock can be made in the microwave cooker when you have a few ingredients available, but larger quantities are best cooked conventionally on a hotplate or burner when they should be simmered for up to 4 hours to extract the full flavour. For convenience, bouillon or stock cubes may be used as alternatives to home-made stocks when time is short, although the finished dish will be somewhat lacking in texture and flavour.

450g (1lb) knuckle of veal or
   chicken bones, cooked or raw
knob of dripping or lard
½ leek, sliced
1 small onion, sliced
1 celery stick, sliced
1 carrot, sliced
1 bouquet garni
¼ × 5ml tsp (¼tsp) salt
6 black peppercorns
1 litre (1¾pt) hot water

White stock (makes about 1 litre/1¾pt)
POWER LEVEL: 100% (FULL) AND 50%

Use when recipes require chicken stock

1 Ask the butcher to cut the veal bones into convenient-sized pieces. Place the veal or chicken bones and dripping or lard into a large bowl, cover and cook on 100% (full) setting for 4 min, turning the bones over halfway through.
2 Add the remaining ingredients, cover and bring to the boil in the microwave (about 10–12 min).
3 Skim the surface of the stock, reduce to 50% setting and continue to cook, covered, for 1 hour, topping up with hot water as necessary.
4 Strain the stock through a sieve or fine muslin, allow to cool then remove the fat from the surface.
5 Use as required, or when cool store in the refrigerator for 2–3 days or freeze.

Cook's note: *The above recipe may be used as chicken broth, providing that chicken bones are used as the basic ingredient*

Brown stock
Use when recipes require beef stock. Follow the recipe for white stock, replacing the veal or chicken bones with marrow bones or shin of beef and adding 1–2 × 15ml tbsp (1–2tbsp) tomato purée to the stock during cooking.

Game stock
Use when recipes require game stock. Follow the recipe for white stock, replacing the veal or chicken bones with game or game bones and trimmings. Add 1 or 2 cloves and 25g (1oz) bacon to the stock.

1·1 litre (2pt) boiling water
350g (12oz) vegetables and
   peelings
salt and freshly ground black
   pepper
bay leaf
blade mace
4 cloves
1 × 15ml tbsp (1tbsp) chopped
   mixed herbs

Vegetable stock (makes about 825ml/1½pt)
POWER LEVEL: 100% (FULL) AND 50%

1 Pour the water into a large bowl or dish and add the mixture of roughly chopped vegetables and peelings, eg onion and skin, carrot, root vegetable peelings, tomato, etc.
2 Add salt, pepper, bay leaf, mace and cloves. Cover and cook for 10 min on 100% (full) and a further 10–15 min on 50% setting.
3 Strain the stock and add the chopped herbs and extra seasoning.
4 Use straight away or cool and store in the refrigerator for 24 hr or freeze.

Fish stock *(makes about 550ml/1pt)*
POWER LEVEL: 100% (FULL) AND 30%

450g (1lb) fish trimmings, washed well
550ml (1pt) water
salt
1 onion, finely chopped
1 stick celery, finely chopped
bouquet garni
6 peppercorns

Use the trimmings of the fish such as bones, head and the skin to make this fish stock. Almost any white fish can be used, but as it does not keep well, the stock should preferably be used on the day it is made

1 Place the fish trimmings in a large bowl or jug with the water and a little salt. Cover and bring to the boil on 100% (full) setting. Remove the bowl and take off any scum from the surface of the water.
2 Add the onion, celery, bouquet garni and peppercorns, cover and cook on 30% setting for 30 min.
3 Strain the stock through a sieve or a fine cloth. Store in the refrigerator until required.

Game soup *(serves 6)*   *colour page 23*
POWER LEVEL: 70%, 100% (FULL) AND 50%

1 pheasant, prepared and trussed
salt and freshly ground black pepper
25g (1oz) butter, melted
450g (1lb) green lentils
1·25 litre (2½pt) boiling game stock (page 20) or water
1 onion, quartered
½ leek, white part only
sprig thyme
1 bay leaf
150ml (¼pt) double cream

This recipe can also be used for any game bird

1 Weigh the pheasant and place breast side down in a casserole dish. Sprinkle lightly with salt and pepper and brush liberally with the melted butter. Cover and cook on 70% setting allowing 11–12 min per ½kg (1lb). Turn the pheasant over breast side up halfway through cooking and baste with the juices. The inner thigh temperature should measure 80–85°C (175–180°F) when using a probe or meat thermometer. Allow to stand for a few minutes.
2 Wash the lentils and place in a large bowl with the game stock or water, onion, leek and herbs. Cover with a lid or pierced clingfilm and cook for 10 min on 100% (full) and a further 15–20 min on 50% setting until tender. Allow the lentils to stand.
3 Carefully slice the breast meat from the pheasant, cut into small dice and reserve. Remove the rest of the meat from the bones and purée it in a food processor or blender.

Stilton Soup (below); Consommé Julienne (below); Game Soup (page 21)

4   Strain the lentils and reserve the liquid. Remove the herbs and purée the lentils and vegetables in the processor or blender with the pheasant meat, adding salt, pepper and enough liquid to moisten the mixture.

5   Combine the purée with the remaining reserved liquid, the diced pheasant and cream. Adjust the seasoning and reheat for 3–4 min on 70% setting before serving.

Cook's note: *225–350g (8–12oz) cooked game can be used in this recipe instead of the fresh pheasant, in which case add it to the lentils 10 min before the end of the cooking. Purée the lentils with the game meat and then proceed as above. A little cooked beef can also be added to give extra meat and texture*

25g (1oz) butter
1 × 15ml tbsp (1tbsp) chopped onion
25g (1oz) flour
425ml (¾pt) boiling chicken stock (page 20)
425ml (¾pt) milk
salt and freshly ground black pepper
pinch each ground bay leaves and cayenne pepper
½ × 5ml tsp (½tsp) mild mustard, optional
175g (6oz) stilton cheese
75ml (⅛pt) single cream
for serving: small croûtons of toasted bread, optional

Stilton soup *(serves 4–6)*   *colour opposite*
POWER LEVEL: 100% (FULL)

1   Heat the butter in a large bowl for 1 min until melted. Add the onion, cover and cook for 1 min.

2   Stir in the flour and then add the chicken stock gradually. Add all the other ingredients except the cheese and cream.

3   Cover and cook for 5 min, stirring twice throughout. Add the cheese and continue to cook for a further 3 min.

4   If preferred the soup may be puréed in a blender or food processor. Reheat in the microwave if necessary.

5   Stir in the cream and serve hot with croûtons of toasted bread if liked.

225g (8oz) lean beef, minced
whites and shells of 2 eggs
salt
½ × 5ml tsp (½tsp) meat extract
1·1 litre (2pt) good hot beef stock (page 20), strained and free of fat
sherry

Consommé *(serves 4)*   *colour opposite*
POWER LEVEL: 100% (FULL) AND 30%

In order to achieve a clear consommé you will need to ensure that all the utensils and cloths are well scalded in boiling water. You will need 3 large bowls, a whisk and a teatowel or fine cloth

1   Place the minced beef into a large bowl or dish. Whisk the egg whites just enough to break them up and add to the bowl with the shells, a little salt and the meat extract. Pour on the hot stock, mixing thoroughly.

2   Cover with a lid and bring to the boil in the microwave on 100% (full) setting, whisking well every 1½–2 min until a froth forms. Do not overboil or the consommé will cloud.

3   Reduce to 30% setting and cook, covered for 1 hr. Strain the liquid through a teatowel or fine cloth twice, using a clean scalded bowl each time. Add a little sherry. The consommé should be a clear, deep amber colour of old sherry.

DO NOT FREEZE

Consommé julienne
Cut 100g (4oz) of mixed carrot, turnip, leek and celery into fine matchsticks and cook in a covered bowl or dish for 3–4 min on 100% (full) setting until tender. Refresh in hot water, place into the serving dish or tureen and pour over the prepared consommé.

Cook's note: *Consommé can also be served chilled, garnished with slices of cucumber. Providing it has been made with a good, home-made beef stock using marrow bone, it will set to a jelly when cooled*

350g (12oz) each of grey mullet, haddock and plaice
6 × 15ml tbsp (6tbsp) olive oil
1 large onion, finely chopped
1 clove garlic, crushed
400g (14oz) can chopped tomatoes
2 × 15ml tbsp (2tbsp) tomato purée
1–2 × 15ml tbsp (1–2tbsp) chopped mixed herbs to taste
825ml (1½pt) boiling fish stock (page 21 and method 1)
150ml (¼pt) dry white wine
1 bay leaf
pared rind 1 lemon
salt and freshly ground black pepper
150ml (¼pt) double cream
for garnish: 8 or 16 large prawns and tomato slices

Mediterranean fish soup *(serves 8)*
POWER LEVEL: 100% (FULL) AND 50%

1 Clean, fillet and skin the fish. Cut the fillets diagonally into 5cm (2in) pieces. The trimmings and bones may be used for stock.
2 Place the oil and onion into a large bowl or dish, mix well together, cover and cook on 100% (full) setting for 4 min. Stir in the garlic and continue to cook for a further 2 min.
3 Add the tomatoes, tomato purée and the herbs, reduce to 50% setting and cook, covered, for 10–12 min. Add the fish, stock, wine, bay leaf and lemon peel and continue to cook for 15 min.
4 Remove the bay leaf, lemon peel and 1 piece of fish for each serving and keep warm. Season the soup and allow to cool slightly.
5 Purée the soup in a blender or food processor or rub through a sieve. Stir in the cream and reheat on 50% setting for 2–3 min, but do not allow it to boil.
6 Peel the prawns, leaving on the heads and tails. Place 1 piece of the reserved fish into each individual bowl and pour over the soup. Garnish with the prawns and tomato slices.

DO NOT FREEZE

1 chicken carcass and trimmings of chicken
1 large onion, chopped
1 carrot, diced
1 leek, sliced
1 bay leaf, crumbled
salt and freshly ground black pepper
825ml (1½pt) boiling chicken stock (page 20) or water
25g (1oz) flaked almonds
1 bunch watercress, washed
150ml (¼pt) milk
150ml (¼pt) double cream
for serving: 3 × 15ml tbsp (3tbsp) double cream

Cream of chicken and watercress soup *(serves 6)*
POWER LEVEL: 100% (FULL)

1 Place the chicken carcass and trimmings, onion, carrot, leek, bay leaf and seasoning into a large bowl. Add the boiling stock or water, cover the bowl and cook for 15–20 min. Leave to cool.
2 Place the almonds onto a heatproof plate and cook for 5–6 min until browned, stirring once throughout cooking. Set to one side.
3 Pick over the chicken, removing all the meat from the bones. Return the meat to the bowl with the stock and vegetables and stir in the watercress and the milk. Cover and cook for a further 15 min, stirring once during cooking.
4 Allow the soup to cool slightly, remove the bay leaf and purée the soup in a blender or food processor. The thickness of the soup will depend on the amount of meat taken from the chicken carcass. If necessary, add a little kneaded butter made from 25g (1oz) of butter and 15g (½oz) flour, and reheat the soup until thickened and boiling.
5 Stir the cream into the soup and adjust the seasoning. Reheat again for 30–60 sec if necessary, not allowing the soup to boil.
6 Pour the soup into a hot dish or tureen and swirl in the extra cream. Sprinkle the browned almonds over the top before serving.

450g (1lb) carrots, sliced
3 oranges, juice and rind
1 onion, chopped
salt and pepper
1 × 5ml tsp (1tsp) grated nutmeg
1 × 15ml tbsp (1tbsp) chopped mint
825ml (1½pt) boiling vegetable stock (page 20)
sugar to taste
1 × 15ml tbsp (1tbsp) soured cream

Carrot and orange soup *(serves 4)*
POWER LEVEL: 100% (FULL)

1 Place the carrots, orange rind and juice and onion in a large bowl. Cover and cook for 8–10 min, stirring once throughout.
2 Add the seasoning, nutmeg, mint and stock. Cover and cook for 10–15 min or until the carrots are tender.
3 Purée the soup in a blender or food processor. Pour the soup into a serving dish.
4 Add sugar to taste and extra seasonings if necessary. Reheat for 2–3 min, stir in the cream and serve hot.

Bisque d'homard *(serves 4–6)*
POWER LEVEL: 100% (FULL) AND 30%

1 In a large bowl or dish melt the butter on 100% (full) setting for 1½ min. Add the carrot, onion and herbs and mix thoroughly. Cover and cook for 5 min.
2 Split the lobsters through from head to tail along the back using a heavy sharp-pointed knife or cleaver. Remove the intestine (a small tube running through the tail), the stomach (the small sac near the head), and the spongy gills.
3 Add the lobster halves to the vegetables, spoon over some of the butter and juices, cover and cook for 3 min.
4 Heat 3–4 × 15ml tbsp (3–4tbsp) brandy for about 1 min until bubbling, pour over the lobsters and ignite. (Do not ignite in the microwave.)
5 Add the wine, stock or water and seasoning and cook, covered, on 30% setting for 15 min. Stir in the rice and continue to cook for a further 20–25 min until the rice is tender.
6 Remove the lobsters from the dish, carefully extract the meat from the shells and dice. Purée the stock, vegetables and rice in a food processor or blender or rub through a sieve. Stir in the cream.
7 Combine the diced lobster meat with the purée and taste for seasoning, adding a little extra brandy if required. Serve hot or chilled.

50g (2oz) butter
1 carrot, finely chopped
1 onion, finely chopped
1 bay leaf
sprig thyme
2 × 15ml tbsp (2tbsp) chopped parsley
2 small cooked lobsters, weighing about 450g (1lb) each
5–6 × 15ml tbsp (5–6tbsp) brandy
275ml (½pt) dry white wine
825ml (1½pt) boiling chicken or fish stock (pages 20 and 21) or water
salt and freshly ground black pepper
100g (4oz) rice, washed
150ml (¼pt) double cream

Hollandaise soup *(serves 4–6)*
POWER LEVEL: 100% (FULL)

1 Place the carrot in a bowl or dish with the salted water and cook, covered, for 3 min. Add the turnip and peas and cook for 4 min. Stir in the cucumber and cook for a further 2 min. Drain the vegetables and keep warm.
2 Melt the butter in a bowl or jug for 1½ min, stir in the flour and add the hot stock gradually, stirring well until thoroughly blended. Cook for 4–5 min until thickened and boiling, stirring every 30–60 sec.
3 Blend the egg yolks and cream, stir into the soup and heat for 1–2 min until thickened without boiling, stirring frequently.
4 Stir the tarragon and sugar into the soup and season to taste with salt and freshly ground black pepper.
5 Drain the vegetables and place into a hot serving dish or tureen. Pour the soup over the vegetables and serve straight away.

DO NOT FREEZE

1 carrot, diced
2 × 15ml tbsp (2tbsp) salted water
1 small turnip, diced
75g (3oz) frozen peas
½ cucumber, deseeded and diced
50g (2oz) butter
50g (2oz) flour
1.1 litre (2pt) hot chicken or vegetable stock (page 20)
2 egg yolks
150ml (¼pt) single cream
1 × 5ml tsp (1tsp) chopped tarragon
½ × 5ml tsp (½tsp) sugar
salt and freshly ground black pepper

Croûtons *(serves 2–3)*
POWER LEVEL: 100% (FULL)

1 Cut the slice of bread into small cubes.
2 Place the butter in a shallow dish and heat for 1 min in the microwave.
3 Add the bread cubes to the dish, toss the bread over in the melted butter and cook, uncovered, for 1 min; turn the bread over and cook for a further 1 min.
4 Drain on kitchen paper towel, allow to stand for 1 min before sprinkling with paprika and serving hot with soup.

1 large, thick slice brown or white bread, crusts removed
25g (1oz) butter
paprika pepper for sprinkling, optional

Cook's note: *This recipe can be doubled to make sufficient croûtons to serve 4–6 people, but for larger quantities it is best to cook conventionally in a frypan or deep-fat fry in oil. If doubling the above quantities, allow an extra 1 min cooking time*

40g (1½oz) butter
2 shallots, finely chopped
½ × 5ml tsp (½tsp) paprika
pinch ground mace
40g (1½oz) flour
425ml (¾pt) milk
salt and freshly ground black
     pepper
12 oysters, fresh or canned
squeeze lemon juice
275ml (½pt) double cream

Oyster soup *(serves 3–4)*
POWER LEVEL: 100% (FULL)

1 Melt the butter in a large bowl for 1–1½ min, stir in the shallots, cover
   and cook for 4–5 min until tender. Add the paprika and mace and cook for
   a further 1 min.
2 Stir the flour into the butter and shallots until well blended and add the
   milk gradually. Season with salt and freshly ground black pepper.
3 Cook, uncovered, for about 6 min until thickened and boiling, stirring
   every minute. The mixture will be quite thick at this stage.
4 Remove the oysters and their juices from the shells, or the canned oysters
   and juices and add to the soup with a squeeze of lemon juice.
5 Stir in the double cream, adjust the seasoning and reheat without boiling
   for 1–2 min, stirring every 30 sec. Serve immediately.

DO NOT FREEZE

450g (1lb) jerusalem artichokes,
     peeled
juice of 1 lemon
50g (2oz) butter
1 onion, finely sliced
1 stick celery, finely sliced
700ml (1¼pt) boiling veal or
     chicken stock (page 20)
150ml (¼pt) dry white wine
bouquet garni
salt and freshly ground black
     pepper
150ml (¼pt) natural yoghurt
150ml (¼pt) double cream
for garnish: chopped chives

Chilled artichoke soup *(serves 6)*
POWER LEVEL: 100% (FULL)

1 Dice the artichokes and leave to soak for 5 min in a bowl of cold water
   with the lemon juice. Drain and pat dry with kitchen paper.
2 Melt the butter in a large dish or bowl for 1½ min, add the artichokes,
   onion and the celery. Toss the vegetables well in the butter.
3 Cover and cook for 3–4 min. Add the boiling stock, wine, bouquet garni
   and seasoning. Cover, bring to the boil in the microwave then continue to
   cook for 10–12 min until the vegetables are tender.
4 Remove the bouquet garni and blend the soup in a food processor or
   liquidiser or rub through a sieve. Adjust the seasoning and leave to cool.
   Chill for 2–3 hr in the refrigerator.
5 Stir in the yoghurt and cream just before serving and sprinkle with
   chopped chives.

DO NOT FREEZE

450g (1lb) black cherries
1 bottle riesling or other
     medium white wine
25–50g (1–2oz) sugar
2·5cm (1in) cinnamon stick
2 lemons
100ml (4fl oz) brandy, optional
550ml (1pt) soured cream
for serving: sponge finger
     biscuits or slices of toasted
     brioche (page 106)

Chilled cherry soup *(serves 4–6)*   *colour opposite*
POWER LEVEL: 100% (FULL) AND 30%

*The unusual contrast of sweet and sharp flavours is the basis for this delicious soup
which can be varied by using other fruits such as apricots or plums*

1 Wash the cherries and stone them, reserving the stones and stalks. Fold
   about half the cherry stones in a cloth and using a heavy weight, crush
   them to expose the kernels.
2 Place the stones, stalks and crushed stones into a large bowl with the
   wine, sugar to taste, cinnamon, grated rind of 1 lemon and the juice from
   both lemons.
3 Cover and bring to the boil on 100% (full), about 6 min, then reduce to
   30% setting and cook for 5 min. Allow to stand for 15 min to infuse the
   flavours.
4 Strain the liquid, return it to the bowl and bring up to the boil again on
   100% (full). Add the cherries including any juice and leave to stand until
   tepid. Stir in the brandy if used.
5 Reserve 1–2 × 15ml tbsp (1–2tbsp) of the soured cream, and place the
   rest in a serving dish and mix in the cherry soup. Refrigerate until chilled.
   Swirl the reserved soured cream into the soup before serving with sponge
   finger biscuits or slices of toasted brioche.

*Jambon à la Crème (page 41);
Chilled Cherry Soup (above);
Turkey and Avocado Salad with
Roquefort Dressing (page 17)*

DO NOT FREEZE

Fish and shellfish

6 large scallops
25g (1oz) butter
salt and pepper
squeeze of lemon juice
6 × 15ml tbsp (6tbsp) double
 cream
4 × 15ml tbsp (4tbsp) browned
 breadcrumbs
for garnish: 4 rashers bacon,
 optional

Scallops baked in cream *(serves 4)*
POWER LEVEL: 100% (FULL)

1 Remove the scallops from their shells, wash and pat dry. Melt the butter for 1 min in the microwave and spoon into 4 scallop shells or individual dishes.
2 Quarter the scallops and divide between the shells or dishes, season lightly and sprinkle with a squeeze of lemon juice. Spoon over the cream.
3 Cover and cook in the microwave for 3–4 min, rearranging the shells or dishes halfway through if necessary. Allow to stand for 3 min.
4 Uncover the scallops and sprinkle with the browned breadcrumbs. Garnish with the bacon rashers which have been grilled or cooked in the microwave until crisp, about 4 min. Serve straight away.

DO NOT FREEZE

675g (1½lb) fillets of brill
3 slices onion
50g (2oz) button mushrooms,
 finely sliced
few sprigs parsley
1 bay leaf
salt and pepper
150ml (¼pt) dry white wine
150ml (¼pt) water
100g (4oz) white or green
 grapes
25g (1oz) butter
25g (1oz) flour
150ml (¼pt) milk,
 approximately
few drops lemon juice
2–3 × 15ml tbsp (2–3tbsp)
 single cream

Brill véronique *(serves 4)*
POWER LEVEL: 100% (FULL)

1 Trim the fillets of brill, wash and pat dry. Arrange them in a large shallow dish with the onion, sliced mushrooms, herbs, seasoning, wine and water.
2 Cover and cook for 5 min. Leave to stand for a few minutes, drain off the stock and reserve.
3 Place the grapes into hot water for a few minutes, then peel, halve and remove the pips. Reserve a few half grapes for decoration.
4 Melt the butter in a large bowl for about 1 min. Stir in the flour until well blended and gradually add the reserved fish stock, made up to 275ml (½pt) with the milk. Cook, uncovered, for 3–4 min until thickened and boiling, stirring every minute. Adjust the seasoning.
5 Stir the grapes, lemon juice and cream into the sauce and pour over the fish. Reheat in the microwave for 3 min before serving, garnished with the reserved grapes.

Alternative fish: lemon or dover sole or plaice

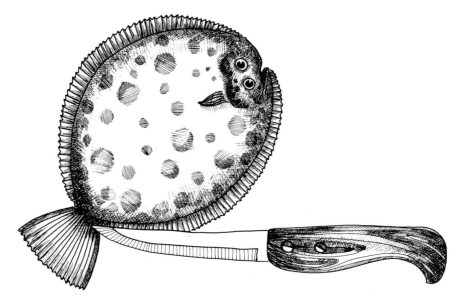

Prawn gougère (serves 3–4)

POWER LEVEL: 100% (FULL)
CONVENTIONAL OVEN TEMPERATURE: 200°C (400°F) MARK 6

1 For the sauce, melt the butter in a covered casserole dish for about 1 min, stir in the onion and cook for 4 min. Add the courgette slices and continue to cook for 1½ min.
2 Stir the 20g (¾oz) flour into the vegetables and gradually add the stock or milk, and seasoning. Cook for 3–4 min, stirring every minute until thickened and boiling. Add the prawns, tomatoes and parsley and adjust the seasoning.
3 For the choux pastry: place the water and butter into a bowl and heat for 3–4 min in the microwave or until boiling well. Quickly add the flour all at once and beat vigorously until blended.
4 When the paste is smooth, add the eggs gradually, beating well after each addition. Stir in the cheddar cheese and season lightly.
5 Place spoonfuls of the choux paste around the sides of a round 20cm (8in) ovenproof gratin dish or pie plate. Fill the centre with the prawn sauce mixture and sprinkle with the parmesan cheese and breadcrumbs.
6 Bake in a preheated oven for 40–50 min until the choux pastry is well risen and brown. Sprinkle well with chopped parsley to garnish before serving straight away.

Alternative shellfish: shrimps, scampi, lobster or crab

20g (¾oz) butter
1 medium onion, finely sliced
1 small courgette, finely sliced, optional
20g (¾oz) flour
275ml (½pt) stock or milk
salt and freshly ground black pepper
225g (8oz) peeled prawns
2 tomatoes, skinned, deseeded and finely chopped
2 × 5ml tsp (2tsp) chopped parsley
1 × 15ml tbsp (1tbsp) grated parmesan cheese
1 × 15ml tbsp (1tbsp) browned breadcrumbs
for garnish: chopped parsley

for the choux pastry:
150ml (¼pt) water
50g (2oz) butter
65g (2½oz) flour
2 eggs, beaten
50g (2oz) cheddar cheese, diced
salt and pepper

Fish pâté (serves 6–8)

POWER LEVEL: 100% (FULL) AND 30%

This pâté has a texture and taste resembling that of lobster, a clever illusion as monkfish is cheaper

1 Place the fish fillets into a dish with the juice of 1 lemon. Chop the flesh of the ½ lemon and scatter it over the fish. Cover the dish and cook on 100% (full) setting for 6–7 min, rearranging the fillets halfway through cooking if necessary. Allow to stand for 5 min before draining off the liquid.
2 Beat the eggs together with the tomato purée and seasoning. Chop the fish into small pieces. Mix with the tomato and egg mixture and pour into a shallow microwave loaf dish.
3 Cover the dish and cook on 30% setting for 15–20 min until set. Allow to cool and then chill in the refrigerator.
4 Turn out onto a serving plate and garnish with sprigs of parsley and the tomato and lemon slices. Serve with mayonnaise handed separately.

675g (1½lb) monkfish, skinned
1½ lemons
4 eggs
150g (5oz) can tomato purée
salt and pepper
for garnish: parsley and tomato and lemon slices
for serving: mayonnaise (page 76)

Scampi à la crème (serves 4–8)   *colour page 31*

POWER LEVEL: 100% (FULL) AND 70%

Serve as a starter or main course

1 Melt the butter in a dish for 1 min, add the scampi, cover and cook on 100% (full) setting for 2 min. Stir in the paprika, cover and cook for 1 min.
2 Heat the sherry for about 30 sec until hot. Remove the cover from the scampi, ignite the sherry and pour over the scampi. Do not ignite in the microwave.
3 Remove the scampi from the dish, return the dish to the microwave and cook, uncovered, for about 4 min to reduce the liquid quantity by half.

25g (1oz) butter
450g (1lb) peeled scampi
1 × 5ml tsp (1tsp) paprika
1 sherry glass dry sherry
3 egg yolks
225ml (8fl oz) double cream
4 tomatoes, skinned, deseeded and diced
salt and freshly ground black pepper
for serving: prebaked individual pastry cases, optional (page 64)

Crab Mousse (below); Scampi à la Crème (page 29); Turban of Sole and Salmon (below)

4   Blend the egg yolks with the cream and add to the dish with the scampi, tomatoes and seasoning. Mix well together.
5   Reduce to 70% setting, cover and cook for 3–4 min until heated through and the sauce has thickened sufficiently to coat the back of a spoon. Stir frequently and do not allow to boil.
6   Adjust the seasoning and serve in individual dishes or prebaked pastry cases as a starter, or with freshly boiled rice and a green salad as a main course.

Alternative fish: prawns, shrimps, lobster, crab or scallops

Crab mousse with cucumber dressing *(serves 8–10)*
POWER LEVEL: 100% (FULL)   *colour opposite*

275ml (½pt) velouté sauce, using 25g (1oz) butter, 25g (1oz) flour and 275ml (½pt) court bouillon (page 32)
450g (1lb) crab meat (½ white, ½ dark approximately)
25g (1oz) gelatin
90ml (3fl oz) dry white wine or water
275ml (½pt) mayonnaise (page 76)
salt and pepper
150ml (¼pt) double cream, whipped
1 cucumber, thinly sliced
salt
4 × 15ml tbsp (4tbsp) french dressing (page 78)
½ × 5ml tsp (½tsp) paprika
few drops tabasco sauce

1   Lightly grease a 17·5cm (7in) soufflé dish, cake tin or mould.
2   In a bowl or dish, melt the butter for the velouté sauce for 1 min, stir in the flour and add the liquid gradually. Cook, uncovered, for about 3 min until thickened, beating the sauce every minute. Add the dark crab meat to the sauce, mix well and leave to cool.
3   Soak the gelatin in the wine or water and then heat for 15–30 sec. Stir well until it is dissolved and add to the cooled velouté sauce with the mayonnaise. Season to taste.
4   Fold the white crab meat and the double cream into the sauce. Pour the mixture into the prepared dish or tin and leave it to set.
5   Place the cucumber slices in a colander and sprinkle generously with salt. Place a plate on the top and leave to degorge for ½–1 hr. Rinse well in cold water and pat the slices dry in kitchen paper.
6   Mix the french dressing with the paprika and tabasco sauce and stir in the cucumber slices.
7   Turn the mousse onto a serving plate or dish. Spoon the cucumber garnish over the top or around the edge of the mousse before serving. Alternatively, serve spoonfuls on individual serving plates and hand the cucumber dressing separately.

DO NOT FREEZE

*450g (1lb) sole fillets, skinned
*450g (1lb) fresh salmon fillets, skinned
1 large egg, beaten
100g (4oz) curd cheese
salt and pepper
75ml (2½fl oz) double cream, lightly whipped
1–2 × 15ml tbsp (1–2tbsp) chopped pistachios
for garnish: watercress
for serving: velouté sauce (page 76) using fish stock (page 21) or court bouillon (page 32)
*Try to choose small, evenly sized thin fillets, or trim to shape

Turban of sole and salmon *(serves 6–8)*   *colour opposite*
POWER LEVEL: 100% (FULL) AND 60%

1   Lightly butter a 17·5cm (7in) microwave ring mould. Line the base and sides of the ring mould with alternate single or double fillets of sole and salmon, overlapping the fillets and using about three-quarters of the fish.
2   Place the remaining fish in a covered dish and cook for 2½–3 min on 100% (full) setting. Cool slightly and then purée with the egg in a food processor or blender, or rub the mixture through a sieve.
3   Beat in the curd cheese, and add seasoning to taste. Gently fold in the double cream and pistachios and mix well together.
4   Spoon the mixture carefully into the prepared ring mould. Smooth the surface with the back of a spoon then fold the fish fillets over the filling.
5   Cover the dish and cook on 60% setting for 9–12 min. Allow the turban to cool. Drain off any surplus liquid and turn the turban out onto a serving plate. Chill well and garnish with sprigs of watercress before serving with the velouté sauce handed separately.

Cook's note: *Any of the following may be incorporated into the filling instead of the pistachios: cooked chopped prawns, shrimps, mushrooms, or chopped truffles*

2 dover sole, each weighing
    about 550–675g (1¼–1½lb),
    skinned and filleted
8 slices lobster meat
    (or 8 scampi)
8 slices truffle, optional
few drops lemon juice
25g (1oz) butter
20g (¾oz) flour
150ml (¼pt) fish stock
    (page 21)
75ml (2½fl oz) double cream
25g (1oz) parmesan cheese,
    grated
salt and pepper

Paupiettes of sole walewska *(serves 4)*   *colour on front cover*
POWER LEVEL: 100% (FULL)
CONVENTIONAL GRILL

1   Wipe or wash the sole fillets and dry. Place a slice of lobster (or 1 scampi)
    and truffle on each fillet and roll up like a swiss roll.
2   Arrange the paupiettes in a circle on a plate, ensuring that the ends of
    the fillets are tucked underneath. Sprinkle with a few drops of lemon
    juice.
3   Cover and cook for 3–4 min and then leave to stand for a few minutes.
    Transfer to a heatproof serving dish and keep warm.
4   Melt the butter in a bowl or jug for 1 min, stir in the flour and when well
    blended gradually stir in the fish stock. Return to the microwave and cook
    for 2½–3 min, stirring every 30 sec until thickened and boiling.
5   Stir the cream into the sauce with three-quarters of the cheese. Add
    seasoning to taste and spoon the sauce over the fish.
6   Sprinkle with the rest of the cheese and glaze the top under a hot grill.

Alternative fish: lemon sole, plaice or brill

40g (1½oz) butter
1 shallot, finely chopped
50–75g (2–3oz) fresh
    breadcrumbs
75–100g (3–4oz) toasted
    hazelnuts, finely chopped or
    ground
1 × 15ml tbsp (1tbsp) chopped
    parsley or dill
salt and freshly ground black
    pepper
1 large egg, beaten
6 salmon cutlets, weighing
    about 175g (6oz) each
juice ½ lemon
for garnish: dill or parsley sprigs
for serving: lemon mayonnaise
    (page 76)

Baked salmon with hazelnut stuffing *(serves 6)*   *colour page 107*
POWER LEVEL: 100% (FULL) AND 70%

1   Melt 15g (½oz) butter on 100% (full) setting for 30 sec in a bowl, stir in
    the shallot, cover and cook for 2–3 min until tender. Add the bread-
    crumbs, hazelnuts, parsley or dill and seasoning to taste. Bind the mixture
    together with the beaten egg.
2   Wipe or wash the salmon cutlets and pat dry. Arrange the 6 cutlets in a
    large shallow dish or place 3 on each of 2 plates.
3   Form the stuffing into 6 portions and press into the cavity of each cutlet.
    Sprinkle with lemon juice, season lightly and dot with the remaining
    butter.
4   Cover and cook on 70% setting for 10–12 min for the 6 cutlets, or 5–6
    min for the 3, turning the dish or rearranging the fish halfway through
    if necessary. Leave to stand for a few minutes before arranging on a
    serving plate.
5   Pipe with a swirl of lemon mayonnaise and garnish with parsley or dill.
    Serve with the rest of the mayonnaise handed separately.

Alternative fish: haddock or cod cutlets

Cook's note: *To toast the hazelnuts in the microwave, place on a heat-resistant
plastic or glass plate and cook, uncovered, on 100% (full) setting for 4–6 min or
until lightly browned*

1 litre (1¾pt) hot water
225g (8oz) carrots, sliced
3 shallots, sliced
1 bay leaf
1 sprig thyme
small bunch parsley
6 peppercorns
75ml (2½fl oz) cider or wine
    vinegar
15g (½oz) salt

Court bouillon *(makes about 1 litre/1¾pt)*
POWER LEVEL: 100% (FULL) AND 50%

Place all the ingredients into a large covered bowl or dish and heat for 10 min
on 100% (full) setting until boiling. Skim, then continue to cook on 50%
setting for 30–45 min. Strain and cool.

Red mullet provençale *(serves 4)*
POWER LEVEL: 100% (FULL)

1 Clean and scale the fish, pierce the eyes and remove gills if desired. Wash well in cold water, and dry with kitchen paper towel. Score the skin and sprinkle the fish with the lemon juice.
2 Heat 2 × 15ml tbsp (2tbsp) oil for 2–3 min until hot. Add the fish in a head-to-tail arrangement, cover and cook for 3 min; turn the fish over in the oil and continue to cook for 2–3 min. Drain and place in a serving dish. Keep warm.
3 Add the remaining oil to the dish with the shallots and garlic, cover and cook for 3–4 min. Add seasoning, tomatoes, parsley and wine, cover and cook for 2–3 min.
4 Pour over the fish, cook for a further 1–2 min to boost serving temperature if necessary.
5 Serve with croûtes of toasted french bread.

Alternative fish: almost any whole fish, steaks or cutlets

4 red mullet
juice ½ lemon
2–3 × 15ml tbsp (2–3tbsp) oil, approximately
2 shallots, finely chopped
1 clove garlic, crushed
salt and freshly ground black pepper
350g (12oz) tomatoes, skinned and chopped, *or* 450g (1lb) can tomatoes
2 × 15ml tbsp (2tbsp) chopped parsley
1 wine glass white wine
for serving: croûtes of toasted french bread

Fish cream newburg *(serves 6–8)*
POWER LEVEL: 100% (FULL) AND 30%

1 Lightly butter a 20–22·5cm (8–9in) microwave ring mould.
2 Prepare a panade by heating the milk on 100% (full) setting with 50g (2oz) butter until the butter is melted and the milk is boiling, about 3½–4 min. Add the flour all at once and beat well until smooth. Add salt and pepper to taste and leave to cool.
3 Blend the fish into the panade and add the beaten eggs and cream. If preferred, the mixture may be blended in a food processor or liquidiser. Adjust the seasoning.
4 Turn the mixture into the prepared ring mould. Cover with pierced cling-film and cook on 30% setting for 18–20 min or until firm to the touch. Allow to stand, covered, while preparing the sauce.
5 Melt the butter in a bowl on 100% (full) setting for 1 min. Add the flour and paprika, beat well and cook for 15 sec. Beat well again and blend in the stock.
6 Return the sauce to the microwave and heat for 2–3 min, stirring every 30 sec until boiling.
7 Heat the prawns or lobster meat in the sherry in a small bowl for 1 min and add to the sauce with the cream. Adjust the seasoning.
8 Turn out the fish cream onto a hot serving plate and spoon over the sauce.

215ml (7½fl oz) milk
50g (2oz) butter
65g (2½oz) flour
salt and pepper
450g (1lb) fresh white fish fillets, skinned and minced or finely chopped
2 eggs, beaten
75ml (2½fl oz) double cream

for the sauce:
25g (1oz) butter
20g (¾oz) flour
½ × 5ml tsp (½tsp) paprika
215ml (7½fl oz) fish stock (page 21)
75g (3oz) peeled prawns or lobster meat
½ sherry glass dry sherry
75ml (2½fl oz) double cream

DO NOT FREEZE

2 small or 1 large cooked lobster
50g (2oz) butter
1 × 15ml tbsp (1tbsp) chopped
    onion
2 × 15ml tbsp (2tbsp) chopped
    parsley
1–2 × 15ml tbsp (1–2tbsp)
    chopped fresh tarragon
4 × 15ml tbsp (4tbsp) white
    wine
275ml (½pt) béchamel sauce
    (page 74)
pinch each dry mustard, salt,
    paprika
3 × 15ml tbsp (3tbsp) grated
    parmesan cheese
2 × 15ml tbsp (2tbsp) browned
    breadcrumbs
slivers of butter
for garnish: watercress

Lobster thermidor (serves 2 or 4)   colour opposite
POWER LEVEL: 100% (FULL)

Live lobsters should be killed by conventional methods and a good fishmonger will usually do this for you. The recipe here uses cooked lobster as the microwave cooker will heat the flesh very quickly ensuring practically no loss of flavour

1   Remove the lobster meat from the shells, discarding the stomach, intestine and spongy-looking gills. Chop the claw and head meat and cut the meat from the tail into thick slices. Wash and dry the shells.
2   Melt 25g (1oz) butter in a large bowl for 1 min. Add the onion, parsley and tarragon, cover and cook for 1 min. Add the wine and cook, uncovered, for 2–3 min until the onion is tender and the liquid quantity is reduced slightly.
3   Stir in the béchamel sauce and mix well with the onion and herbs. Add the lobster meat, seasonings, remaining butter and 2 × 15ml tbsp (2tbsp) of the cheese. Cover and heat for 2–3 min.
4   Divide the mixture between the shells. Sprinkle with the remaining cheese, and breadcrumbs, and top with slivers of butter. Cook, uncovered, for 1½–2 min until hot through or alternatively brown the top under a hot grill.
5   Serve straight away garnished with watercress.

DO NOT FREEZE

4 turbot steaks, 675g (1½lb)
    approximately
few drops lemon juice
salt and pepper
few sprigs parsley
1 bay leaf
150ml (¼pt) white wine
25g (1oz) butter
25g (1oz) flour
150ml (¼pt) milk,
    approximately
75–100g (3–4oz) crab meat,
    flaked
25g (1oz) parmesan cheese,
    grated
paprika for sprinkling
for garnish: parsley sprigs

Turbot with crab sauce (serves 4)
POWER LEVEL: 100% (FULL)

1   Wash and dry the fish, place in a shallow casserole dish with the lemon juice, seasoning, herbs and wine. Cover and cook for 7–9 min until tender, rearranging the fish halfway through if required. Drain off, reserve and measure the stock.
2   Melt the butter in a bowl for 1 min and stir in the flour. Make the liquid quantity of the reserved stock up to 275ml (½pt) with the milk and gradually stir this into the butter and flour. Cook for 3–4 min until cooked and thickened, stirring every 30 sec.
3   Stir in the crab meat and cook for a further 1–2 min. Adjust the seasoning and spoon the sauce over the turbot.
4   Sprinkle with parmesan cheese and paprika and heat through, uncovered, for 1–2 min. Alternatively, brown under a hot grill. Garnish with a little parsley and serve hot.

Alternative fish: steaks of halibut, cod or haddock

1 × 675g (1½lb) halibut steak
salt and freshly ground black
    pepper
juice ½ lemon
75g (3oz) butter
2 leeks
1 × 5ml tsp (1tsp) paprika
100g (4oz) peeled prawns

Halibut steak dieppoise (serves 4)
POWER LEVEL: 100% (FULL)

1   Wipe or wash the fish and pat dry. Place in a shallow dish, season with a little salt and pepper and sprinkle with the lemon juice.
2   Melt 50g (2oz) of the butter in a small cup or jug for 1½ min and pour over the fish. Cover and cook for 6–7 min, turning the dish halfway through if necessary. Leave to stand, covered.
3   Slice the white part of the leeks into rounds and shred the green parts. Melt the remaining butter for 1 min, add the white leek rounds, cover and cook for 3 min. Add the paprika and prawns and continue to cook for a further 2–3 min.
4   Place the shredded green leeks onto a plate, cover and cook for 2–3 min until just softened, shaking or stirring the dish once throughout. Combine

Lobster Thermidor (above)

the leek mixtures and add salt and freshly ground black pepper.

5   Carefully remove the skin and bone from the halibut and drain off the liquid. Spoon the topping over the fish and serve straight away.

Alternative fish: individual steaks of cod, hake, haddock

Trout with cucumber *(serves 4)*
POWER LEVEL: 100% (FULL) AND 70%

75g (3oz) butter
1 cucumber, thinly sliced
4 trout, weighing 200–225g (7–8oz) each, cleaned and gutted
salt and freshly ground black pepper
2 × 15ml tbsp (2tbsp) dry white wine or white wine vinegar

This dish may be served hot or cold

1   In a large shallow ovenware dish, melt 25g (1oz) butter in the microwave on 100% (full) setting for 1 min. Remove the heads and score the skin at the thickest part of the fish.

2   Layer half the cucumber in the base of the dish, arrange the trout head to tail on the top and cover with the remaining cucumber slices.

3   Sprinkle with a little salt and black pepper and the white wine or wine vinegar. Top with 25g (1oz) of the butter cut into slivers, cover and cook on 70% setting for 15–18 min, rearranging the fish halfway through if necessary.

4   Leave to stand for a few minutes then remove the trout and cucumber from the dish onto a serving platter.

5   Strain the juices through a fine sieve and boil in the microwave on 100% (full) setting for 2 min, uncovered. Add the rest of the butter cut into pieces and stir until dissolved. Return the dish to the microwave and continue to boil until the liquid has been reduced by about half and resembles a glaze.

6   Pour the glaze over the trout and serve straight away or leave to cool.

Alternative fish: mackerel

DO NOT FREEZE

Cod gourmet *(serves 4–6)*
POWER LEVEL: 100% (FULL)

675–900g (1½–2lb) cod fillet, skinned
salt and freshly ground black pepper
squeeze of lemon juice
150ml (¼pt) water
1 shallot or small onion, finely chopped
1 wine glass white wine
25g (1oz) butter, softened
15g (½oz) flour
1–2 × 15ml tbsp (1–2tbsp) double cream
2 × 5ml tsp (2tsp) freshly chopped parsley
2 tomatoes, skinned, deseeded and cut into thin shreds
for garnish: toasted or fried croûtes of french bread

1   Wipe or wash and pat dry the fish and cut the fillets if necessary into serving portions. Place into a large shallow dish with the thinner ends of the fish towards the centre of the dish.

2   Sprinkle with a little salt and pepper and a squeeze of lemon juice. Add the water, cover and cook for 7–10 min, turning the dish or rearranging the fish halfway through. Drain and reserve the liquid.

3   Place the shallot or onion and wine into a bowl, bring to the boil in the microwave and cook, uncovered, for about 4–5 min until the liquid quantity is reduced by half.

4   Blend the butter and flour together and stir into the wine and onion mixture. Add the reserved fish stock and cook for 2–3 min, stirring every minute until thickened and boiling. Add the cream, parsley and tomatoes and heat through for 1–1½ min. Adjust the seasoning to taste.

5   Pour the sauce over the cod and serve hot, garnished with toasted or fried croûtes of french bread.

Alternative fish: any white fish fillet

Meat entrées

Gigot of lamb with redcurrant glaze *(serves 8–10)* *colour page 11*
POWER LEVEL: 100% (FULL) AND 70%
CONVENTIONAL GRILL

450g (1lb) redcurrants, stringed
50g (2oz) butter
50–100g (2–4oz) sugar
150ml (¼pt) red wine
1 long leg of lamb with chump,
   weighing about 2kg (4lb)
2 bay leaves
black pepper

1 Place the redcurrants, butter, sugar to taste and wine in a covered dish and cook on 100% (full) setting for 6–8 min, stirring once during cooking.
2 Rub the sauce through a sieve and replace in the dish. Cook, uncovered, for 10–15 min until well reduced, stirring once or twice throughout.
3 Place half the sauce into a serving jug and set the remainder to one side to be used as a glaze.
4 Trim the lamb and weigh. Make some slits in the meat, break the bay leaves and place a little in each slit, rubbing the flesh gently with your fingers to extract the flavour from the bay.
5 Season the fat side of the lamb with black pepper and protect the knuckle by wrapping with a smooth piece of aluminium foil.
6 Place the lamb fat side down on a microwave roasting rack or trivet and cook on 70% setting, allowing 11–13 min per 450g (1lb), covering with kitchen paper towel if preferred to prevent splashing. Turn the joint over halfway through and finish the cooking period with the fat side uppermost. Remove the foil halfway through.
7 Brush the lamb with the redcurrant glaze. Preheat a conventional grill to a medium heat and brown the lamb slowly, turning the meat as necessary and continuing to brush with the glaze until it is all used.
8 Stand for 5 min, then carve and serve with the redcurrant sauce handed separately.

Braised beef flamande with tomatoes *(serves 6)*
POWER LEVEL: 100% (FULL), 30% AND 70%

450g (1lb) mixed root
   vegetables, eg onion, carrot,
   turnip, parsnip
3 × 15ml tbsp (3tbsp) water
1¼kg (2½lb) joint topside
150ml (¼pt) boiling beef stock
   (page 20)
150ml (¼pt) brown ale
1 × 15ml tbsp (1tbsp) tomato
   purée
freshly ground black pepper
bouquet garni
1 × 15ml tbsp (1tbsp) olive oil
1 spanish onion, finely sliced
450g (1lb) tomatoes, skinned
   and chopped
salt
2 × 15ml tbsp (2tbsp) butter
   kneaded with 1 × 15ml tbsp
   (1tbsp) flour

1 Peel and prepare the vegetables by slicing or dicing into small pieces. Place them into a large casserole dish with the water, cover and cook on 100% (full) setting for 5–6 min, stirring once.
2 Place the beef on the vegetables. Mix together the stock, ale and tomato purée, season with black pepper and pour over the beef, adding the bouquet garni.
3 Cook the beef, covered, for 1–1½ hr or until tender on 30% setting. Turn the beef joint over once halfway through cooking. Allow to stand.
4 Heat the oil in a bowl for 1 min on 100% (full), add the onion and cook, covered, for 3–4 min. Stir in the tomatoes and cook uncovered, for 4–5 min or until the tomatoes are softened. Season to taste with salt and black pepper.
5 Remove the beef from the casserole dish onto a chopping board and cut into slices. Arrange the tomato sauce on a serving plate and lay the slices of beef on the top.
6 Remove and disgard the vegetables and bouquet garni from the casserole. Add the kneaded butter to the gravy and blend well. Heat, uncovered, on 100% (full) for 4–5 min or until thickened and adjust the seasoning.
7 Reheat the beef and tomatoes for 4–5 min on 70% setting or until piping hot. Serve with the gravy handed separately.

Cook's note: *Tie the beef into a neat shape with string before cooking*

50g (2oz) butter
2 sticks celery, chopped or
    finely sliced
3 carrots, diced
1 onion, diced
2 cloves garlic, crushed
1¼kg (2½lb) shin of veal, cut
    into slices 5cm (2in) thick
2 × 15ml tbsp (2tbsp) seasoned
    flour
1 × 400g (14oz) can chopped
    tomatoes
225ml (8fl oz) dry white wine
275ml (½pt) boiling veal or
    chicken stock (page 00),
    approximately
salt and freshly ground black
    pepper
sprig rosemary, chopped

for the risotto milanèse:
40g (1½oz) unsalted butter
1 marrow bone
1 onion, chopped
150ml (¼pt) dry white wine
450g (1lb) italian rice
½ × 5ml tsp (½tsp) powdered
    saffron
1·1 litre (2pt) boiling veal or
    chicken stock (page 20)
40g (1½oz) unsalted butter
75g (3oz) parmesan cheese,
    grated

for garnish: 4 × 15ml tbsp
    (4tbsp) chopped parsley
2 lemons, grated rind
2 cloves garlic, finely chopped

Ossi buchi with risotto milanèse *(serves 6)*   *colour opposite*
POWER LEVEL: 100% (FULL) AND 30%

1   Melt the 50g (2oz) butter in a casserole dish for 2 min, add the prepared vegetables and garlic and cook, covered, for 4–6 min on 100% (full) setting, stirring once during cooking.
2   Toss the veal in the seasoned flour, add to the casserole dish, cover and cook for 6 min. Stand the pieces of veal on their sides to prevent the marrow falling out of the bone, and rearrange once during cooking.
3   Add the tomatoes to the dish and stir in the white wine. Add sufficient boiling stock to cover then add the seasoning to taste and the rosemary.
4   Cover the dish and cook for 10 min on 100% (full) and a further 30–40 min on 30% setting. Keep warm.
5   Heat 40g (1½oz) butter in another casserole dish for 1½ min on 100% (full) and add the marrow from the bone and the chopped onion. Cover and cook for 4–5 min, stirring once throughout. Add the 150ml (¼pt) white wine and cook, uncovered, for 4–5 min until reduced by about half.
6   Add the rice and cook for 3 min, stirring once. Add the saffron and the stock. Cover and cook for 18–20 min and allow to stand for 5 min.
7   Remove the slices of veal from the dish and strain the liquid through a conical strainer, pressing through the tomato but retaining the vegetables.
8   Stir the remaining butter, cut into slivers, into the rice and add the parmesan. Season to taste with salt and pepper. Place the rice onto a large serving plate and arrange the veal on top.
9   If the tomato sauce from the veal is thin, reduce it until syrupy by cooking in the microwave, uncovered, on 100% (full) setting for about 10 min. Reheat the ossi buchi if necessary for 3–4 min.
10   Pour the sauce over the meat and garnish with the parsley, lemon rind and chopped garlic, mixed together.

olive oil
4 thin escalopes of veal,
    weighing about 50g (2oz)
    each
6 × 15ml tbsp (6tbsp) brown
    ginger wine
juice of ½ lemon
3 × 15ml tbsp (3tbsp) double
    cream
salt and freshly ground black
    pepper
for garnish: twists of lemon or
    lime

Escalopes of veal with ginger wine *(serves 2)*
POWER LEVEL: 100% (FULL)

1   Preheat a large browning dish for 5–6 min. Brush the surface lightly with olive oil and then add the veal. Press the escalopes down well with a heat-proof spatula and cook for 2 min. Turn the pieces of veal over and cook for a further 1–2 min. Leave the veal on the browning dish to keep warm, but strain the meat juices into a measuring jug.
2   Add the ginger wine to the meat juices and heat for 2–3 min, uncovered, until reduced and syrupy. Add the lemon juice and cream and heat for a further 2–3 min before seasoning to taste with salt and freshly ground black pepper.
3   Place the veal onto a hot serving plate or dish and spoon over the ginger sauce. Garnish with twists of lemon or lime before serving.

Ossi Buchi with Risotto Milanèse
(above)

1½kg (3lb) corner gammon
water
25g (1oz) butter
2 onions, chopped
2 sticks celery, finely sliced
2 carrots, diced
1 small turnip, diced
150ml (¼pt) madeira
275ml (½pt) boiling chicken
   stock (page 20)
bouquet garni

for the sauce:
2 × 15ml tbsp (2tbsp) olive oil
1 × 15ml tbsp (1tbsp) flour
550ml (1pt) boiling stock (see
   method 5)
2 × 5ml tsp (2tsp) tomato purée
150ml (¼pt) madeira
salt and freshly ground black
   pepper
for garnish: chopped parsley
for serving: fresh cooked spinach

Braised ham with madeira *(serves 8)*
POWER LEVEL: 100% (FULL), 50% AND 70%

1 Soak the gammon overnight in cold water and drain. Place in a casserole dish and cover with boiling water. Cover and par-cook by allowing 4–5 min per 450g (1lb) on 100% (full) setting. Leave to stand.
2 Melt the butter in a large dish for 1–2 min, add the prepared vegetables and cook, covered, for 4–6 min, stirring once.
3 Drain the gammon and place it on top of the vegetables. Heat the madeira for 1–2 min until hot, remove from the microwave and ignite. Pour the flaming madeira over the gammon and add the boiling stock and bouquet garni.
4 Cover and cook for 10–12 min per 450g (1lb) on 50% setting, turning the gammon over halfway through. Allow to stand while making the sauce.
5 Heat the oil for 2 min on 100% (full) setting, add the flour and cook for 30–60 sec. Gradually add the stock, using some of the braising liquid if not too salty. Add a few of the braising vegetables from around the gammon and the tomato purée. Cook, uncovered, for about 30 min until thickened.
6 While the sauce is cooking, remove the rind from the gammon and slice the meat.
7 Place the madeira in the microwave and heat for 5–8 min on 100% (full) setting until it has reduced by about half. Rub the sauce through a coarse sieve, add the madeira and seasoning to taste.
8 Reheat the sliced gammon on a serving plate, covered, for 5–6 min on 70% setting until hot. Pour the sauce over the gammon and garnish with parsley before serving with fresh cooked spinach.

Cook's note: *Tie the gammon joint with string to help retain a neat shape during cooking*

Jambon à la crème (*serves 4–6*)   *colour page 27*
POWER LEVEL: 100% (FULL) AND 70%
CONVENTIONAL GRILL

175g (6oz) mushrooms,
  trimmed and sliced
175ml (6fl oz) dry white wine
4 shallots, chopped
8 thick slices cooked york ham
50g (2oz) butter
2 × 15ml tbsp (2tbsp) flour
275ml (½pt) double cream
450g (1lb) tomatoes, skinned
  and chopped
salt and freshly ground black
  pepper
50g (2oz) parmesan cheese,
  grated
for garnish: tomato slices,
  optional

1 Place the mushrooms in a dish with the wine and cook, uncovered, on 100% (full) setting for 5 min. Remove the mushrooms from the dish using a draining spoon and reserve.
2 Add the shallots to the wine and cook for 10–12 min, uncovered, until the wine has evaporated.
3 Arrange the slices of ham in a large shallow dish and sprinkle the mushrooms over them.
4 Melt the butter in a bowl for 2 min, add the flour and stir well. Gradually add the cream and then add the shallots and tomatoes. Season with salt and freshly ground black pepper.
5 Spoon the sauce over the ham and heat, covered, on 70% setting for 5 min.
6 While heating the ham, preheat a conventional grill.
7 Sprinkle the parmesan cheese over the dish and brown under the grill. Garnish with tomato slices if liked and serve immediately.

Pork chops ardennaise (*serves 4*)
POWER LEVEL: 100% (FULL) AND 70%

2 thick gammon rashers,
  weighing about 100g (4oz)
  each
1 small onion, finely chopped
150ml (¼pt) white wine
4 lean pork chops or steaks,
  weighing about 225g (8oz)
  each
40g (1½oz) butter
1 × 15ml tbsp (1tbsp) flour
150ml (¼pt) double cream
1 × 5ml tsp (1tsp) french
  mustard
salt and freshly ground black
  pepper
for garnish: chopped parsley

1 Cut the gammon rashers into julienne strips and place in a bowl. Add the chopped onion and the wine and leave to marinate for 30 min. Remove the gammon and the onion from the wine using a draining spoon and reserve them separately.
2 Preheat a large browning dish for 6 min, add the chops and cook for 4 min at 100% (full), turn them over and cook for a further 8–10 min on 70% setting. Leave on the dish to keep warm.
3 Melt the butter in a large dish for 1–2 min on 100% (full), add the onion and gammon, cover and cook for 4 min, stirring once. Sprinkle the flour into the dish and stir well. Add the reserved wine and cook for 3–4 min, stirring every minute until thickened. Add the cream and heat for 3–4 min on 70% setting, not allowing it to boil. Stir the mustard into the sauce and season to taste.
4 Place the chops on a hot serving plate and pour the sauce over. Garnish with chopped parsley and serve with a crisp salad including some orange segments.

Calves' liver with dubonnet and orange (*serves 4*)
POWER LEVEL: 100% (FULL)

675g (1½lb) calves' liver
2 × 15ml tbsp (2tbsp) seasoned
  flour
25g (1oz) butter
1 × 15ml tbsp (1tbsp) olive oil
1 large onion, finely chopped
1 clove garlic, finely chopped
1 orange, grated rind and 1 ×
  15ml tbsp (1tbsp) juice
8 × 15ml tbsp (8tbsp) red
  dubonnet
salt and freshly ground black
  pepper
1 lemon, grated rind
2 × 15ml tbsp (2tbsp) chopped
  parsley
for garnish: chopped parsley

1 Trim the liver and cut into slices. Toss the liver in the seasoned flour.
2 Heat the butter and the oil in a large shallow dish for 2–3 min until the butter has melted, add the onion and the garlic, cover and cook for 3–4 min, stirring once throughout.
3 Add the liver and cook for 6–7 min, covered, until just cooked. Rearrange the slices of liver during cooking if necessary.
4 Transfer the liver to a warmed serving plate, remove the onions from the dish with a draining spoon and place over the liver.
5 Add the orange juice and dubonnet to the meat juices in the dish and add seasoning to taste. Cook for 5–8 min, uncovered, until reduced by half. Add the grated lemon and orange rinds and the parsley and pour the sauce over the liver.
6 Reheat if necessary for 2–3 min and serve garnished with chopped parsley.

2 × 15ml tbsp (2tbsp) olive oil
40g (1½oz) butter
3 shallots or 1 small onion,
  finely chopped
1 clove garlic, finely chopped
900g (2lb) porterhouse or
  sirloin steak, cut into 5cm
  (2in) cubes
1 × heaped 15ml tbsp (1 heaped
  tbsp) wholewheat flour
275ml (½pt) boiling beef stock
  (page 20)
2 × 15ml tbsp (2tbsp) tomato
  purée
salt and freshly ground black
  pepper
225g (8oz) button mushrooms
150ml (¼pt) white wine
for garnish: chopped fresh
  parsley

Beef sauté chasseur *(serves 6)*   *colour opposite*
POWER LEVEL: 100% (FULL), AND 30%

1 Put the oil and 25g (1oz) butter in a large casserole dish and heat for 1–2 min on 100% (full) setting until the butter is melted. Add the shallots or onion and garlic, cover and cook for 2 min.
2 Stir in the beef and cook, covered, for 6 min, stirring once throughout. Remove the meat from the dish using a draining spoon.
3 Add the flour to the dish, mix well to blend and cook for 1 min. Stir in the boiling stock gradually and add 1 × 15ml tbsp (1tbsp) tomato purée. Cook, uncovered, for 4–5 min, stirring every minute until boiling and thickened.
4 Return the beef to the casserole, season, cover and cook for 40 min on 30% setting or until tender. Stir once during cooking.
5 Allow the casserole to stand, covered, while preparing the mushrooms. Trim the mushrooms and halve any large ones.
6 Heat the rest of the butter in a bowl for 30sec or until melted, add the mushrooms and wine and cook, uncovered, on 100% (full) setting for 8–10 min.
7 Add the mushrooms and wine to the casserole dish with the rest of the tomato purée and stir well. Cover the dish and heat for 5 min or until piping hot. Adjust the seasoning and serve garnished with chopped parsley.

8 noisettes of lamb
1 onion, chopped
1 carrot, diced
2 sticks celery, diced
25g (1oz) lean bacon
25g (1oz) flour
275ml (½pt) dry red wine
550ml (1pt) boiling stock
  (page 20)
1 × 15ml tbsp (1tbsp) tomato
  purée
bouquet garni
1 sprig fresh rosemary
2–3 × 15ml tbsp (2–3tbsp)
  redcurrant jelly
salt and freshly ground pepper

Noisettes of lamb shrewsbury *(serves 3–4)*   *colour opposite*
POWER LEVEL: 100% (FULL) AND 70%

1 If you have a good butcher, ask him to prepare the noisettes for you. Alternatively, have the butcher chine 2 best ends of lamb and remove the rib bones. Trim the meat, roll up and tie securely at about 2·5cm (1in) intervals. Cut into slices between the string.
2 Place the vegetables in a casserole dish with the bacon and any trimmings from the lamb. Cover and cook for 8–10 min on 100% (full) setting, stirring once halfway through.
3 Add the flour to the vegetables, stir well and cook, uncovered, for 1 min. Gradually add the wine, boiling stock and tomato purée. Finally add the bouquet garni and the rosemary.
4 Cook, uncovered, for about 20 min on 100% (full) setting until reduced and thick enough to coat the back of a spoon.
5 Preheat a large browning dish for 6 min. Add the noisettes and cook for 4 min on the first side, turn and cook for a further 4–6 min on 70% setting. Alternatively cook under a conventional grill until browned and tender.
6 While the noisettes are cooking remove the bouquet garni from the sauce and rub the sauce through a coarse sieve. Add the redcurrant jelly and season to taste with salt and freshly ground pepper.
7 Place the noisettes onto a warmed serving dish. Reheat the sauce if necessary and pour a little over the noisettes before serving with the rest of the sauce handed separately. Alternatively, pour the sauce in a thin layer onto individual serving plates and arrange the noisettes on top.

Chou-fleur Polonais (page 65); Beef Sauté Chasseur (above); Noisettes of Lamb Shrewsbury (above)

900g (2lb) lambs' sweetbreads
salt
tepid water
275–425ml (½–¾pt) hot
    chicken stock (page 20)
2 × 5ml tsp (2tsp) lemon juice
    or white wine vinegar
4 dessert apples
100g (4oz) butter
4 ripe bananas
sugar and lemon juice to taste
2 × 15ml tbsp (2tbsp) seasoned
    flour
2 × 15ml tbsp (2tbsp) brandy
1 × 15ml tbsp (1tbsp)
    arrowroot
2 × 15ml tbsp (2tbsp) double
    cream
for garnish: chopped parsley

Sweetbreads à la castillane *(serves 4–6)*
POWER LEVEL: 100% (FULL) AND 70%

1   Prepare the sweetbreads for cooking as given below in Cook's note.
2   Trim any fat and tubes from the sweetbreads but leave the thin skins intact. Cut them into 12mm (½in) slices.
3   Peel, core and slice the apples and place them in a dish with 50g (2oz) of butter. Cook, covered, on 100% (full) setting for 8–10 min until soft, stirring once or twice during cooking. Peel and slice the bananas, add to the apple and blend or process the fruits to a smooth purée. Add a little sugar and lemon juice to taste.
4   Melt the rest of the butter in a casserole dish for 1–2 min. Toss the sweetbreads in the seasoned flour and add to the butter. Cover and cook for 6–8 min, stirring once throughout.
5   Add 275ml (½pt) of the reserved stock to the dish, stir well and cook for 15 min, uncovered, stirring once or twice throughout.
6   Place the fruit purée onto a serving plate. Remove the sweetbreads from the cooking liquid with a draining spoon and place them onto the fruit purée.
7   Add the brandy to the cooking liquid. Blend the arrowroot with a little of the liquid, then add to the dish and cook the sauce for 4–5 min, stirring every minute, until thickened.
8   Reheat the sweetbreads and purée for 5 min on 70% setting. Meanwhile season the sauce and stir in the cream.
9   Garnish the dish with chopped parsley and serve with the sauce handed separately.

Cook's note: *Lamb sweetbreads are good alternatives to calf sweetbreads which are traditionally used for this recipe but are sometimes difficult to obtain and can be expensive.*

To prepare lamb sweetbreads for cooking, soak them in the salted tepid water for 1 hr then drain. Cover with the chicken stock, add the lemon juice or vinegar, cover the dish and bring to the boil on 100% (full) setting. Cook for 1 min and leave to stand for 3–5 min. They will lose their pink, raw look. Drain off and reserve 275ml (½pt) stock

8 lambs' kidneys
25g (1oz) butter
3 shallots, finely chopped
1 × heaped 15ml tbsp (1 heaped
    tbsp) flour
275ml (½pt) boiling chicken
    stock (page 20)
1 × 15ml tbsp (1tbsp)
    redcurrant jelly
1 × 15ml tbsp (1tbsp) dijon
    mustard
2 × 15ml tbsp (2tbsp) double
    cream
1 × 15ml tbsp (1tbsp) sherry
salt and freshly ground black
    pepper

Lambs' kidneys gourmet *(serves 2–3)*
POWER LEVEL: 100% (FULL) AND 60%

1   Skin the kidneys, remove the cores and cut the kidneys into small pieces.
2   Melt the butter in a casserole dish for 1 min, add the kidneys, stir well and cook on 100% (full) setting for 4 min, stirring once throughout. Remove the kidneys and put to one side.
3   Add the shallots to the meat juices, cover and cook for 2–3 min, stirring once during cooking. Stir in the flour until well blended and gradually add the boiling stock. Heat for about 4 min until boiling, stirring every minute.
4   Blend the redcurrant jelly, mustard, cream and sherry into the sauce. Season well with salt and freshly ground black pepper and stir the kidneys into the sauce.
5   Reheat for 5–8 min, covered, on 60% setting until piping hot and serve straight away.

Cook's note: *Ensure all the core is removed from the kidney to prevent it bursting during cooking*

Steak, kidney and oyster pie (serves 8)

POWER LEVEL: 100% (FULL) AND 30%
CONVENTIONAL OVEN TEMPERATURE: 190°C (375°F) MARK 5

1 Place the onion in a large covered casserole dish with the butter. Cook for 3 min on 100% (full) setting, stir well, add the kidney and steak and continue to cook for 6–8 min, stirring once.
2 Dredge the flour over the meat and mix well together. Gradually add the stout and stir in seasoning and add the bay leaf. Cover and cook for 10 min on 100% (full) and a further 45-50 min or until tender on 30% setting. Allow to cool.
3 Remove the bay leaf from the dish. Add the drained oysters and the mushrooms to the meat and transfer to a large pie dish.
4 Make the pastry: place the flour into a bowl with a pinch of salt. Cut the butter into small pieces and rub it into the flour. Add the egg yolk and sufficient water to make a stiff dough. Knead lightly on a floured surface and roll out to fit the top of the pie.
5 Place a pastry strip around the lip of the pie dish and brush with water. Cover the dish with the pastry and trim off the excess, making it into pastry leaves to decorate the top. Dampen the underside of the leaves before placing them on the pastry. Seal and crimp the edges of the pie. Make a small slit in the centre of the pastry.
6 Bake in the preheated oven for 30–40 min until the pastry is cooked and golden brown.

1 large onion, sliced
15g (½oz) butter
225g (8oz) lambs' kidneys, skinned, cored and chopped
675g (1½lb) lean braising steak, cubed
2 × 15ml tbsp (2tbsp) flour
425ml (¾pt) stout
salt and pepper
1 bay leaf
1 × 90g (3½oz) can smoked oysters, drained
175g (6oz) mushrooms, sliced

for the pastry:
175g (6oz) plain flour
100g (4oz) butter
1 egg yolk
water

Steak au poivre (serves 4)

POWER LEVEL: 100% (FULL)

1 Trim the steaks and press the crushed peppercorns well into the surface on both sides of the steaks.
2 Preheat a large browning dish for 6 min. Add the oil and the steaks and press them down on the hot surface with a heatproof spatula. Cook for 2 min, turn the steaks over, press down again and then cook for a further 3 min. Leave the steaks on the browning dish to keep warm.
3 Pour any juices from the browning dish into an ovenproof bowl and add the butter. Heat until the butter has melted, about 1–2 min. Add the

4 fillet steaks, weighing about 175g (6oz) each
2 × 15ml tbsp (2tbsp) black peppercorns, coarsely crushed
1 × 15ml tbsp (1tbsp) olive oil
50g (2oz) unsalted butter
2 × 15ml tbsp (2tbsp) brandy
150ml (¼pt) double cream
salt

brandy and heat for 30–60 sec until hot and bubbling. Remove from the microwave and ignite.
4   Allow the flames to die down and stir the cream into the sauce. Season the sauce with salt and heat for 30–60 sec.
5   Place the steaks onto a hot serving plate and pour the sauce over. Serve straight away.

50g (2oz) butter
1 onion, finely sliced
1 small piece fresh ginger, peeled and grated
900g (2lb) pork tenderloin
2 × 15ml tbsp (2tbsp) seasoned wholewheat flour
175g (6oz) button mushrooms, sliced
salt and freshly ground black pepper
100ml (4fl oz) brandy
150ml (¼pt) soured cream
for garnish: parsley sprigs

Tenderloin of pork with mushrooms in soured cream *(serves 6)*
POWER LEVEL: 100% (FULL)

1   Melt the butter in a large shallow dish for 1–2 min, stir in the onion and ginger, cover and cook for 2–3 min.
2   Trim the tenderloins and cut into small slices, about 12mm (½in) thick. Toss the pork in the seasoned flour.
3   Add the pork to the dish and cook, covered with kitchen paper towel, for 10–12 min. Stir well. Add the mushrooms and cook for a further 6–8 min.
4   Season well to taste with salt and freshly ground black pepper.
5   Heat the brandy for 1 min until bubbling, remove from the microwave, ignite and, while flaming, pour onto the pork.
6   Stir in the soured cream and serve garnished with parsley.

1 × 15ml tbsp (1tbsp) ghee (or clarified butter or oil)
3 × 15ml tbsp (3tbsp) coriander seeds, crushed
1 aubergine, about 225g (8oz)
1 khol rhabi, about 275g (10oz)
1 small sweet potato, about 225g (8oz)
1 green chilli, finely diced
piece root ginger, peeled and grated
grated rind of 1 lemon
1 onion, sliced
2 cloves garlic, crushed
900g (2lb) lamb neck fillet, trimmed and diced
2 × 15ml tbsp (2tbsp) flour
275ml (½pt) boiling chicken or white stock (page 20)
275ml (½pt) red wine
2 × 15ml tbsp (2tbsp) tomato purée
1–2 × 5ml tsp (1–2tsp) coriander seeds
salt and pepper
½–1 × 5ml tsp (½–1tsp) chilli powder
2 × 15ml tbsp (2tbsp) soured cream

Spiced Fillets of Lamb (above) and Spiced Chick Peas and Sweet Potato (page 84); Almonds and Cashew Biriani (page 88) with Vegetable Curry (page 88)

Spiced fillets of lamb *(serves 6)*   *colour opposite*
POWER LEVEL: 100% (FULL) AND 50%

1   Heat the ghee or clarified butter or oil in a small bowl on 100% (full) setting for 1 min, add the coriander seeds and cook for 2–3 min.
2   Halve and slice the aubergine, peel and dice the khol rhabi and the sweet potato, and place in a large casserole dish with the chilli, ginger, lemon rind, onion and garlic. Cover and cook for 10–12 min, stirring once throughout.
3   Add the lamb to the vegetables, cover and cook for 6–8 min stirring once during cooking. Sprinkle the flour over the meat and stir well.
4   Blend together the stock, wine and tomato purée and gradually add the liquid to the casserole dish, stirring well. Add the coriander seeds, salt and pepper and chilli powder.
5   Cover and cook for 10 min on 100% (full) and a further 45–50 min on 50% setting, stirring once or twice during cooking.
6   Adjust the seasoning and stir in the cream before serving hot.

Cook's note: *Although clarified butter or oil can be used for this recipe, it does not have the distinctive flavour of ghee*

Poultry and game

6 chicken breasts
1 small onion, sliced
1 sprig thyme
4 sprigs parsley
small bay leaf
6 peppercorns
275ml (½pt) hot water or
   chicken stock (page 20)
pinch salt
275ml (½pt) aspic jelly (page
   109, or use powdered aspic)
2 × 5ml tsp (2tsp) powdered
   gelatin
275ml (½pt) mayonnaise
   (page 76)
for garnish: peel from cucumber,
   lemon and orange, thin strips
   of red pepper

Chaud-froid of chicken (*serves 6*)   *colour page 79*
POWER LEVEL: 100% (FULL) AND 30%

This classic french dish uses whole cooked chicken which is coated with an aspic sauce and elaborately decorated. Chicken breasts are easier to handle and in this recipe I have used a mayonnaise sauce as a base, although a béchamel or velouté could be used instead

1   Wipe the chicken breasts and place in a large shallow casserole dish, arranging them in an even layer. Add the onion, herbs, peppercorns, hot water or stock and pinch of salt.
2   Cover the dish and cook on 100% (full) setting for 5–6 min until boiling. Reduce to 30% setting and simmer for 40–50 min until the chicken is tender, carefully rearranging the portions twice throughout. Lift the chicken from the dish, leave to drain and cool.
3   (If powdered aspic is being used, make it up to the directions on the packet.) Add a little of the aspic to the gelatin, heat for 15–30 sec on 100% (full) setting, stir well until dissolved, and then stir into the rest of the aspic jelly.
4   Allow the aspic to stand until almost set and blend half into the mayonnaise.
5   Carefully remove the skin from the chicken and trim the pieces into an even shape. Place the chicken on a wire rack over a large plate or tray to catch the drips.
6   Coat each piece of chicken carefully with the aspic sauce, allowing any excess to run off. Leave in a cool place for 15–20 min to set.
7   Garnish the chicken attractively with shapes cut from the peel, using tiny aspic cutters and a sharp knife. Dip the shapes into the remaining aspic before placing on the chicken.
8   Carefully spoon over any remaining aspic and leave in a cool place to set completely.

DO NOT FREEZE

Cook's note: *Should the aspic jelly start to set before the chicken is coated, melt it by warming slightly in the microwave, allowing 1–2 min on 30% setting until runny. Stir well before using*

350–450g (¾–1lb) streaky
   bacon, derinded
1 small pheasant, weighing
   about 900g (2lb), boned
225g (8oz) chicken breast
2 onions
2 cloves garlic, crushed
100g (4oz) belly pork
grated rind of 1 orange
salt and freshly ground black
   pepper
½ × 5ml tsp (½tsp) ground
   mace
1 × 15ml tbsp (1tbsp) chopped
   parsley
85ml (3fl oz) red wine
for garnish: orange butterflies
   and parsley sprigs

Pheasant and chicken terrine (*serves 8*)
POWER LEVEL: 60%

Serve as a starter

1   Line a 17·5cm (7in) microwave ring mould or round dish with the rashers of bacon, leaving the ends of the rashers to fold over the top of the filled mould.
2   Finely mince together the pheasant meat, chicken, onion, garlic and belly of pork. Add all the remaining ingredients except the garnish and mix well.
3   Carefully spoon the mixture into the prepared dish. Fold the ends of the bacon over the filling, adding extra pieces if necessary to enclose the terrine.
4   Cook for 20–25 min or until the juices run clear when a skewer is inserted into the terrine. Place a plate over the mould and press under a heavy weight in the refrigerator overnight.
5   Turn out onto a serving platter and garnish with orange butterflies and sprigs of parsley.

Goose ballotine (serves 8–10) *colour page 19*

POWER LEVEL: 100% (FULL) AND 50%

This recipe for boned and stuffed goose can also be used to prepare and cook a small turkey. By halving the amount of stuffing, a 2–2¹⁄₂kg (4–5lb) duck or chicken can be cooked in a similar way

1. Ask the butcher to bone the goose for you. Trim away any excess fat and skin and discard. Use the bones and giblets to make a good stock.
2. For the stuffing, melt the butter in a large bowl for 1 min on 100% (full) setting. Stir in the onion, cover and cook for 3 min. Add the rest of the ingredients for the stuffing, finally binding the mixture together with the beaten egg.
3. Fill the goose with the stuffing and sew up neatly using a trussing needle and fine string. Tie at intervals of 5cm (2in) along the length of the bird. Place the goose breast side down on a microwave roasting rack. Protect the ends of the bird with aluminium foil.
4. Cook on 50% setting for 1¹⁄₄–1¹⁄₂ hr, turning the goose over halfway through cooking. Baste occasionally with the juices and pour off excess liquid from the dish as necessary throughout cooking. When done, the juices from the centre of the meat should run clear or the centre of the meat measure a temperature of 80°C (175°F) when using a probe or meat thermometer. Wrap the goose in foil and leave to stand. Skim off the fat and juices from the dish but reserve the meat sediment.
5. For the sauce, place the oil in a large bowl with the prepared vegetables and large mushroom. Mix well together, cover and cook for 6 min on 100% (full) setting. Stir in the flour and cook for a further 1 min. Add the stock gradually, stir in the sediment from the meat and mix well. Add the tomato purée to give a good, rich colour, the sherry, seasoning and bouquet garni. Cover and cook on 50% setting for 20 min. Strain the sauce and add the button mushrooms. Continue to cook for 5 min.
6. Serve the goose whole or in slices. Pour over a little of the sauce and serve the rest separately. Garnish with tomato, cucumber or watercress before serving.

1 goose, weighing about 5kg (10lb), boned

for the stuffing:
25g (1oz) butter
1 onion, finely chopped
675g (1¹⁄₂lb) pork or veal, minced or grounded in a food processor
75g (3oz) fresh breadcrumbs
1 × 15ml tbsp (1tbsp) each chopped fresh parsley and sage
salt and freshly ground black pepper
1 sherry glass medium-dry sherry
175g (6oz) lean cooked ham, shredded
40g (1¹⁄₂oz) pistachio nuts or walnuts, chopped
1 egg, beaten

for the sauce:
3 × 15ml tbsp (3tbsp) oil
1 carrot, finely diced
1 stick celery, finely diced
1 small onion, chopped
1 large mushroom, chopped
40g (1¹⁄₂oz) flour
550ml (1pt) stock, made from the goose bones and giblets
1–2 × 15ml tbsp (1–2tbsp) tomato purée
1–2 sherry glasses medium-dry sherry
salt and freshly ground black pepper
bouquet garni
175g (6oz) button mushrooms, sliced
for garnish: tomato, cucumber or watercress

Salmi of grouse (serves 2–4)

POWER LEVEL: 100% (FULL), 50% AND 30%

Salmi is a cooking method of lightly roasting the birds before cooking in a rich sauce made with a good stock and flavoured with wine

1. Place the stock, wine and crushed juniper berries into a large bowl or jug. Chop the livers and add to the stock with the giblets. Cover the dish, bring to the boil on 100% (full) setting then reduce to 50% and cook for 15 min.
2. Place the prepared grouse into a large casserole dish. Protect the legs and wing tips with small pieces of aluminium foil and cover the breasts with the fat bacon rashers. Cook, uncovered, on 50% setting for 10 min. Remove the grouse from the dish and cut into halves.

425ml (³⁄₄pt) veal or chicken stock (page 20)
2 wine glasses red wine
12 juniper berries, crushed
2 grouse, with giblets
4–6 rashers fat bacon
25g (1oz) butter
1 shallot, finely chopped
25g (1oz) flour
salt and freshly ground black pepper
100g (4oz) button mushrooms, thickly sliced

for garnish: chopped parsley and toasted or fried breadcrumbs

3   Add the butter to the dish and melt on 100% (full) for 1 min. Stir in the shallot, cover and cook for 2 min. Stir in the flour and cook, uncovered, for 5 min until lightly browned.

4   Strain the stock and add to the roux gradually, add seasoning to taste and cook for 3 min until thickened and boiling. Replace the grouse in the dish and top with the mushrooms. Spoon over some of the sauce, cover with a lid and cook on 30% setting for 45–60 min until tender.

5   Serve sprinkled with chopped parsley and toasted or fried breadcrumbs.

Fricassée of rabbit *(serves 4–6)*   *colour opposite*
POWER LEVEL: 100% (FULL) AND 30%

15g (½oz) butter
100g (4oz) bacon rashers, derinded and cut into strips
2 onions, finely sliced
675g (1½lb) boned rabbit
15g (½oz) flour
salt and freshly ground black pepper
275ml (½pt) hot veal or chicken stock (page 20)
bouquet garni
1 bay leaf
150ml (¼pt) double cream
1–2 × 5ml tsp (1–2tsp) mild mustard
for garnish: chopped fresh chives

1   Melt the butter in a large casserole dish for 30 sec on 100% (full) setting. Add the bacon and onions, stir well, cover and cook for 6 min stirring well once during cooking.

2   Cut the rabbit into small cubes and add to casserole dish. Stir well, cover and cook for 4 min.

3   Mix in the flour and seasoning. Add the stock gradually, mix well together and add the bouquet garni and bay leaf.

4   Reduce to 30% setting and cook, covered, for 50–60 min until tender, stirring 2–3 times throughout. Allow to stand for 15 min.

5   Mix the cream with the mustard and stir into the casserole. Adjust the seasoning to taste.

6   Remove the bouquet garni and bay leaf and reheat the dish for 2–3 min if necessary before serving sprinkled with chopped chives.

Pigeons en cocotte *(serves 4)*   *colour opposite*
POWER LEVEL: 100% (FULL) AND 30%

4 pigeons
50g (2oz) butter
50g (2oz) mushrooms, chopped
squeeze lemon juice
175g (6oz) veal or pork, minced
50g (2oz) tongue, chopped
salt and freshly ground black pepper
40g (1½oz) butter
1 sherry glass medium-dry sherry, approximately
400g (14oz) can chopped tomatoes
150ml (¼pt) chicken or veal stock (page 20)
for garnish: watercress

1   Cut the pigeons down the back and remove the bones from the back and carcass.

2   Melt 50g (2oz) butter for 1½–2 min, add the mushrooms and cook, covered, for 2 min on 100% (full) setting. Add a good squeeze of lemon juice, the minced veal or pork and the tongue. Season to taste and mix well together.

3   Fill the pigeons with the stuffing, sew up neatly with a trussing needle and fine string.

4   Melt the 40g (1½oz) butter in a casserole dish just large enough to take the pigeons, for 1–1½ min. Add the pigeons to the dish, brush with the butter and cover and cook for 2 min.

5   Heat the sherry until bubbling, about 1 min, pour over the pigeons and ignite. Do not ignite in the microwave. Add the tomatoes and stock to the dish, season lightly, cover and cook for 1½–2 hr. Turn the pigeons over in the sauce 4 times throughout.

6   Lift the pigeons from the casserole onto a hot serving dish and keep warm. Purée the sauce in a blender or processor, adding a little more sherry if required.

7   Boil the sauce in the microwave, uncovered, for about 10 min until slightly reduced. Stir 2–3 times throughout the cooking. Pour the sauce over the pigeons and garnish with watercress before serving.

Fricassée of Rabbit (above); Salmi of Grouse (page 49); Pigeons en Cocotte (above)

1 duck, weighing 2–2½kg
   (4½–5lb) with giblets
salt and freshly ground black
   pepper
2 dessert apples, peeled, cored
   and quartered
10–12 prunes, soaked and
   stoned (see page 10)
3–4 × 15ml tbsp (3–4tbsp)
   chopped fresh mixed herbs
1 onion, sliced
275ml (½pt) chicken stock
   (page 20)
1–2 × 15ml tbsp (1–2tbsp) flour,
   blended with a little stock
3–4 × 15ml tbsp (3–4tbsp)
   soured cream
for serving: almond croquettes
   (page 70)

Duck with herbs (*serves 4*)   *colour page 15*
POWER LEVEL: 70% AND 100% (FULL)

The duck is cooked in the microwave and browned in a hot oven or under a grill

1 Wipe the prepared duck and dry the skin if necessary with kitchen paper
   towel. Sprinkle inside and out with salt and pepper and rub well into the
   skin.
2 Place the apples and prunes inside the duck with 1 × 15ml tbsp (1tbsp) of
   the herbs. Fasten the cavity and neck openings if necessary with wooden
   cocktail sticks or skewers. Protect wings and drumsticks with smooth
   pieces of aluminium foil.
3 Arrange the duck, breast side down, on a microwave roasting rack and
   cook on 70% setting allowing 9–11 min per ½kg (1lb). When done the
   juices should run clear and the inner thigh temperature should measure
   80–85°C (175–180°F) when using a probe or meat thermometer. Turn the
   duck over, breast side up, halfway through cooking.
4 Remove the foil pieces and sprinkle the duck with the remaining herbs.
   Slowly brown the surface of the duck in a hot oven or under a medium-hot
   grill.
5 While the duck is browning, prepare the gravy. Skim off the fat from the
   duck juices and place 275ml (½pt) of the juices and meat sediment into a
   large jug or bowl with the onion, chicken stock, giblets and seasoning.
6 Cover and cook on 100% (full) setting for 10 min. Skim the surface of the
   gravy then thicken with the flour blended with a little stock. Bring the
   gravy to the boil again and then strain. Stir in the soured cream and adjust
   the seasoning to taste.
7 Serve the duck on a hot serving platter with the almond croquettes
   arranged around the duck. Hand the sauce separately.

Cook's note: *The ducks now reared in certain regions of France – sometimes
referred to as Barbary ducks – are ideal for microwave cooking as there is much less
fat in the bird and the breast meat is considerably increased*

1 hare, jointed
275ml (½pt) brown ale
1 clove garlic, crushed
1 bay leaf
2 large onions, finely sliced
½ × 5ml tsp (½tsp) grated
   nutmeg
freshly ground black pepper
1–2 × 15ml tbsp (1–2tbsp)
   french mustard
40g (1½oz) butter
150ml (¼pt) stock
1 × 15ml tbsp (1tbsp) plain
   flour
salt
75ml (2½fl oz) double cream
for serving: creamed potatoes
   (page 72)

Braised hare in beer (*serves 4*)
POWER LEVEL: 100% (FULL) AND 30%

The hare is marinated overnight before cooking to remove some of the strong flavour

1 Wipe the hare and place in a large bowl with the ale, garlic, bay leaf,
   onions, nutmeg and black pepper. Leave in the refrigerator or cool place
   overnight.
2 Remove the joints of hare from the marinade and pat dry with kitchen
   paper towel. Spread the joints with the mustard.
3 Melt the butter in a large casserole dish for 1–2 min, add the hare and
   brush with the butter. Cook, uncovered, on 100% (full) setting for 2 min,
   turn the joints over and cook for a further 2 min.
4 Stir in the stock and marinade, cover the dish and bring to the boil in the
   microwave, about 5–6 min. Reduce to 30% setting and cook for 1½hr
   until tender, turning the hare joints halfway through.
5 Lift the hare joints from the dish onto a hot serving plate or dish. Skim off
   some of the fat from the liquid and blend with the flour.
6 Stir the blended flour into the gravy, bring to the boil on 100% (full)
   setting, stirring every minute until thickened and boiling. Remove the
   bay leaf.
7 Adjust the seasoning to taste with salt and black pepper and stir in the
   cream. Spoon the sauce over the hare before serving with creamy mashed
   potatoes.

Poulet à la suisse (serves 6)   colour page 71
POWER LEVEL: 50% AND 100% (FULL)
CONVENTIONAL GRILL

1 large onion, thinly sliced
2 large carrots, thinly sliced
1 stick celery, thinly sliced
6 chicken breasts, skinned
6 thin rashers streaky bacon
150ml (¼pt) hot chicken stock
  (page 20)
bouquet garni
65g (2½oz) butter
40g (1½oz) flour
425ml (¾pt) milk, infused with
  1 slice onion, 6 peppercorns,
  1 bay leaf and 1 blade mace
  (see béchamel sauce, page 74)
50g (2oz) gruyère cheese,
  grated
3–4 × 15ml tbsp (3–4tbsp)
  double cream
salt and freshly ground black
  pepper
225–350g (8–12oz) egg noodles
1 × 15ml tbsp (1tbsp) oil
boiling water
15g (½oz) parmesan cheese,
  grated
for garnish: parsley

1 Place the onion, carrots and celery in a large casserole dish. Arrange the chicken breasts on the top with the thinner ends towards the centre of the dish. Place a bacon rasher on top of each chicken breast.
2 Pour the chicken stock onto the dish and tuck the bouquet garni in with the vegetables. Cover and cook on 50% setting for 30–40 min until the chicken is tender and the juices run clear. Leave to stand and keep the dish warm.
3 Melt 40g (1½oz) butter in a large bowl or jug for 1–1½ min on 100% (full) setting. Stir in the flour and add the strained milk gradually. Mix well together and cook for 3–4 min until thickened and boiling, stirring every minute.
4 Strain off 150ml (¼pt) stock from the chicken and vegetables and stir into the sauce. Beat in the gruyère cheese and finally stir in the double cream and add seasoning to taste. Keep the sauce hot.
5 Place the egg noodles into a large bowl, add 1 × 5ml tsp (1tsp) salt and the oil and cover with boiling water. Cover the dish and cook on 100% (full) setting for 6–7 min or until just tender.
6 Drain the noodles and refresh in hot water. Stir in the remaining butter and some freshly ground black pepper and place into a hot shallow serving dish.
7 Remove the bacon from the top of the chicken and discard. Lift the chicken breasts from the dish and arrange over the noodles.
8 Reheat the sauce if necessary and beat well. Spoon the sauce over the chicken and sprinkle with the parmesan cheese. Lightly brown the top of the dish under a hot grill before serving, garnished with parsley.

DO NOT FREEZE

Casserole of pheasant (serves 4)
POWER LEVEL: 100% (FULL) AND 30%

25g (1oz) butter
2 pheasants
1 spanish onion, finely chopped
100g (4oz) lean bacon rashers,
  derinded and cut into strips
1 × 15ml tbsp (1tbsp) flour
275ml (½pt) red wine,
  approximately
150ml (¼pt) chicken stock
  (page 20)
1 × 15ml tbsp (1tbsp) tomato
  purée
1 × 15ml tbsp (1tbsp) sugar
salt and freshly ground black
  pepper
1 bay leaf
bouquet garni
225g (8oz) button mushrooms,
  wiped or washed
kneaded butter made with 25g
  (1oz) softened butter and 20g
  (¾oz) flour
4 × 15ml tbsp (4tbsp) double
  cream
for garnish: chopped parsley

1 Melt the butter in a large deep casserole dish on 100% (full) setting for 1 min. Add the pheasants to the dish and brush with the butter. Cover and cook for 2 min, turn the pheasants over and continue to cook for a further 2 min.
2 Lift the pheasants from the dish onto a plate. Stir the onion and bacon into the dish, cover and cook for 5 min.
3 Stir in the flour, wine, chicken stock, tomato purée, sugar, seasoning, bay leaf and bouquet garni. Cover and cook for 5 min until thickened and boiling, stirring twice throughout.
4 Add the pheasants to the dish, ensuring that they are well covered with the liquid. If not, add a little more wine or stock to the dish. Reduce to 30% setting, cover and cook for 1¼–1½ hr, turning the dish or rearranging the pheasants halfway through.
5 Add the mushrooms to the dish, stirring them into the sauce with the kneaded butter. Mix well together and continue to cook for a further 10 min. Leave to stand for 20 min. Remove the bay leaf and bouquet garni.
6 Stir in the cream, reheat the dish if necessary for 1–2 min before serving garnished with chopped parsley.

1 chicken weighing 1¾–2kg
    (3½–4lb)
25g (1oz) butter
2 × 15ml tbsp (2tbsp) olive oil
175g (6oz) button onions,
    peeled
boiling water
100g (4oz) gammon rashers, cut
    into strips
150–275ml (¼–½pt) burgundy
275ml (½pt) boiling chicken
    stock (page 20)
2 cloves garlic, crushed
salt and freshly ground black
    pepper
bouquet garni
kneaded butter made with 25g
    (1oz) softened butter and 20g
    (¾oz) flour
for garnish: fried croûtes french
    bread and chopped parsley

Coq au vin *(serves 4–6)*   *colour opposite*
POWER LEVEL: 100% (FULL) AND 30%

The chicken is lightly browned in a frying pan before jointing and cooking in the microwave oven

1   Tie or truss the chicken neatly and lightly brown by frying slowly in the butter and oil.
2   While the chicken is browning, place the onions in a bowl and cover with boiling water. Cover the dish and cook in the microwave on 100% (full) setting for about 3 min until the water is boiling. Allow to stand for 3 min then drain.
3   Lift the chicken from the frypan and add the drained onions and gammon. While these are browning, cut the chicken into joints.
4   Heat 150ml (¼pt) burgundy in a jug in the microwave for 1½–2 min. Replace the chicken in the frypan, pour over the wine and ignite.
5   Transfer the chicken to a suitable microwave casserole dish and top with the onions, gammon and wine from the frypan. Add the stock, garlic, seasoning and bouquet garni and add a little more wine if necessary. Cover the dish with a lid.
6   Cook on 30% setting for 50–60 min or until tender and the chicken juices run clear. Lift the chicken with a draining spoon and arrange on a hot serving dish. Remove the bouquet garni and stir the kneaded butter into the sauce.
7   Cook, uncovered, on 100% (full) setting for 2–3 min until thickened and boiling, stirring every minute. Adjust the seasoning and pour the sauce over the chicken. Garnish with fried croûtes of french bread and sprinkle with chopped parsley before serving.

Cook's note: *If you find it easier, joint the chicken before lightly browning in the frypan*

2 partridges
25g (1oz) butter
2 × 15ml tbsp (2tbsp) olive oil
2 dessert apples, ie cox's, sliced
2–3 shallots, finely sliced
salt and pepper
1 bay leaf
bouquet garni
2 × 15ml tbsp (2tbsp) flour
150ml (¼pt) cider
2 × 15ml tbsp (2tbsp) calvados
kneaded butter made from 25g
    (1oz) softened butter and 15g
    (½oz) flour
75ml (2½fl oz) double cream
for garnish: chopped parsley

Partridges normande *(serves 2–4)*
POWER LEVEL: 100% (FULL) AND 30%

1   Wipe the partridges, place into a large casserole dish with the butter and oil. Cover and cook on 100% (full) setting for 8 min, turning the birds over halfway through.
2   Remove the partridges from the dish, cover and keep warm. Add the apples, shallots, seasoning, bay leaf and bouquet garni to the dish and mix well together.
3   Cover and cook for 10 min, stirring twice throughout. Blend the flour with a little of the cider and add to the dish with the rest of the cider. Bring to the boil, about 3 min, add the calvados and arrange the partridges in the dish.
4   Reduce to 30% setting and cook for about 60 min until tender. Lift the partridges from the dish and cut each in half. Remove the bay leaf and bouquet garni from the liquid and rub the sauce through a sieve or purée in a blender or food processor. Adjust the seasoning.
5   Boil the sauce on 100% (full) setting and thicken with a little kneaded butter. Bring to the boil again and stir in the cream. Spoon the sauce over the partridges before serving garnished with chopped parsley.

*Coq au Vin (above); Wild Rice,
Mushroom and Shrimp Salad with
Aïoli (page 16)*

40g (1½oz) butter
1 spanish onion, finely chopped
50g (2oz) cooked ham or lean
    bacon, derinded and diced
1 chicken, 1½–2kg (3–4lb),
    with giblets
salt and freshly ground black
    pepper
4 × 15ml tbsp (4tbsp) calvados
    or brandy
2 × 5ml tsp (2tsp) finely
    chopped celery leaves
275ml (½pt) unsweetened
    apple juice or still cider
2 large egg yolks
150ml (¼pt) double cream
for garnish: 2 dessert apples,
    peeled, cored and cut into
    6mm (¼in) rings
15g (½oz) butter, melted

Poulet à la crème *(serves 4–6)*
POWER LEVEL: 100% (FULL) AND 70%

From Normandy, this recipe for casserole of chicken includes cream and calvados or brandy to produce the rich sauce

1   Melt the butter in a large casserole dish on 100% (full) setting for 1–1½ min. Stir in the onion and ham or bacon, cover and cook for 4 min.
2   Wipe the prepared chicken and sprinkle inside and out with a little salt and black pepper. Protect the wings and drumsticks with small, smooth pieces of aluminium foil.
3   Place the chicken into the dish breast downwards and baste with the onion and ham or bacon mixture. Cook, uncovered, for 2 min, turn the chicken over, breast side up, and continue to cook for 2 min.
4   Heat the spirit in the microwave for about 1 min until bubbling, pour over the chicken and ignite. Do not ignite in the microwave.
5   Add the celery leaves to the dish with the apple juice or cider and the neck and gizzard from the giblets (omit the liver).
6   Reduce to 70% setting and cook, covered, for 27–40 min (allow 9–10 min per ½kg/1lb). The inside thigh temperature should measure 80–85°C (175–180°F) when using a probe or meat thermometer. Turn the chicken over in the juices 3–4 times during cooking and baste well with the liquid.
7   Remove the foil from the chicken, lift the bird onto a hot serving dish and keep hot. Strain the juices and boil in the microwave on 100% (full) setting for 5–7 min until slightly reduced. Skim off any fat from the surface.
8   Beat together the egg yolks and cream and add a little of the hot stock. Stir into the rest of the stock and cook on 70% setting for 2–3 min until thickened but do not allow to boil. Stir 2–3 times throughout. Adjust the seasoning to taste.
9   Arrange the apple rings for the garnish on a plate and brush with the melted butter. Cover and cook on 100% (full) for about 2 min until tender.
10 Just before serving, pour the hot sauce over the chicken (remove the skin if preferred) and garnish with the apple slices.

DO NOT FREEZE

25g (1oz) butter
175g (6oz) button mushrooms,
    thinly sliced
salt and freshly ground black
    pepper
4 escalopes of turkey, about
    100g (4oz) each
20g (¾oz) seasoned flour
4 slices lean cooked ham
4 slices bel paese or gruyère
    cheese
1 × 15ml tbsp (1tbsp) olive oil
1 × 15ml tbsp (1tbsp) melted
    butter
1–2 × 15ml tbsp (1–2tbsp)
    chopped parsley
4–6 × 15ml tbsp (4–6tbsp) hot
    chicken stock (page 20)
for garnish: parsley sprigs or
    watercress

Escalopes of turkey cordon bleu *(serves 4)*
POWER LEVEL: 100% (FULL) AND 50%

1   Melt the butter in a small dish or bowl for 1 min on 100% (full) setting and stir in the button mushrooms. Season lightly and cook, uncovered, for 2½–3 min. Leave on one side.
2   Wipe the escalopes and coat them in the seasoned flour. Trim the ham and cheese slices to the shape of the escalopes.
3   Heat a large browning dish in the microwave for 6 min. Add the olive oil and melted butter and brush over the surface of the dish.
4   Quickly arrange the turkey pieces in the dish, press down with a heat-proof spatula for about 10 sec, then cook, uncovered, on 100% (full) setting for 3 min. Turn the pieces over and cook for a further 3 min.
5   Place a slice of ham on each escalope, spoon over the mushrooms and sprinkle with parsley. Top with the slices of cheese.
6   Pour the stock into the dish and cook, covered, for 5 min on 50% setting until the cheese is melted.
7   Lift the escalopes with a draining spoon onto a hot serving dish. Garnish with sprigs of parsley or watercress and serve hot.

Egg and cheese dishes

Poached eggs hollandaise *(serves 6)*
POWER LEVEL: 70%

This recipe can be varied in different ways to provide alternative dishes. For example, tomato cups or toasted bread cases (page 64) can be used for serving instead of individual flan cases. A purée of vegetables could be prepared as a bed for the eggs instead of the parma ham, and a cheese or anchovy sauce topping instead of the hollandaise

boiling water
6 eggs
75g (3oz) parma ham, cut into strips
6 baked individual pastry cases (page 64)
salt and pepper
hollandaise sauce (page 77)

1 Pour the boiling water into 6 individual cups, ramekin dishes or small bowls to a depth of about 2·5cm (1in). Break an egg into each dish, prick the yolks and arrange the dishes in a circle on the microwave cooker shelf.
2 Cook, uncovered, for 4–5 min on 70% setting until the eggs are just set. Allow to stand for a few minutes.
3 Arrange the parma ham in the baked pastry cases. Using a draining spoon, remove the eggs from their dishes and arrange them on top of the ham. Sprinkle with seasoning to taste.
4 Coat the eggs with spoonfuls of hollandaise sauce and serve warm.

DO NOT FREEZE

Variation: *Poached eggs with anchovy sauce (page 74): colour page 75*

Omelette basque *(serves 2–4)*
POWER LEVEL: 100% (FULL) AND 50%

2 × 15ml tbsp (2tbsp) olive oil
1 onion, chopped
1 green pepper, deseeded and cut into strips
1 clove garlic, crushed
4 tomatoes, skinned and quartered
50–75g (2–3oz) jambon de bayonne, or cooked lean ham, diced
4–6 eggs
2 × 15ml tbsp (2tbsp) cream, optional
salt and freshly ground black pepper
for garnish: chopped parsley

1 Place the olive oil in a 20cm (8in) round, shallow dish with the onion. Mix well together, cover and cook for 2 min on 100% (full) setting. Add the pepper and garlic, stir well and continue to cook for 2 min. Mix in the tomatoes and ham and cook for a further 2 min.
2 Beat the eggs with the cream and seasoning to taste. Pour over the vegetables and ham in the dish and cook for 1 min on 100% (full) setting. Draw the edges of the omelette together with a spoon or spatula, cover with a lid and continue to cook on 50% setting for 8–10 min until the omelette is set.
3 Sprinkle with the chopped parsley and serve in wedges straight from the dish.

DO NOT FREEZE

Scrambled egg croustades *(serves 6)*
POWER LEVEL: 100% (FULL)

6 eggs
6 × 15ml tbsp (6tbsp) double cream
salt and freshly ground black pepper
25g (1oz) butter, cut into slivers
100g (4oz) peeled shrimps or prawns
6 prebaked individual flan cases (page 64)
for garnish: chopped parsley, unpeeled shrimps or prawns, and lemon twists

1 Beat the eggs in a bowl with the cream, seasoning and butter. Cook, uncovered, in the microwave for 4–5 min, stirring well every 45 sec.
2 Add the peeled shrimps or prawns and continue to cook, stirring gently for a further 1–2 min until the eggs are set and creamy.
3 Spoon the eggs into individual flan cases and serve straight away garnished with a little chopped parsley, an unpeeled shrimp or prawn and a lemon twist.

DO NOT FREEZE

75g (3oz) button mushrooms, thinly sliced
few drops lemon juice
15g (½oz) butter, softened
150ml (¼pt) double cream
6 eggs
salt and freshly ground black pepper
grated nutmeg
100g (4oz) gruyère cheese, grated

Egg with mushrooms à la crème *(serves 6)*
POWER LEVEL: 100% (FULL) AND 70%

1 Place the mushrooms in a bowl, sprinkle with a few drops of lemon juice and add the butter. Cook, uncovered, on 100% (full) setting for 1½min, stirring once throughout. Drain and keep warm.
2 Spoon half the cream between 6 individual ramekin dishes. Break an egg into each dish and prick the yolks with the pointed end of a sharp knife. Arrange the drained mushrooms over the eggs.
3 Mix the rest of the cream with a little seasoning and a pinch of nutmeg and spoon it over the mushrooms. Top with the grated gruyère cheese.
4 Arrange the ramekins in a circle on the microwave cooker shelf and cook, uncovered, on 70% setting for 6–8 min until the eggs are set, popping them back for an extra 15 sec at a time if necessary. Turn the dishes once during cooking.
5 Sprinkle with a little grated nutmeg before serving or alternatively brown the tops of the dishes under a hot grill.

DO NOT FREEZE

for the flan pastry:
250g (9oz) plain flour
salt
175g (6oz) butter, cut into pieces
½ large egg, size 1 or 2, beaten

for the filling:
450g (1lb) very ripe brie, crust removed
150ml (¼pt) double cream
150ml (¼pt) milk
4 eggs, beaten
1 × 5ml tsp (1tsp) ground ginger
½ × 5ml tsp (½tsp) powdered saffron dissolved in 1 × 5ml tsp (1tsp) water
salt
¼–½ × 5ml tsp (¼–½tsp) demerara sugar or grated nutmeg, optional
for garnish: cucumber slices, optional

Brie tart *(serves 6–8)*   *colour opposite*
POWER LEVEL: 100% (FULL) AND 30%
CONVENTIONAL GRILL

1 Sift the flour with a pinch of salt and rub in the butter. Mix in the egg and knead the dough together lightly. If using a food mixer, place all the ingredients for the pastry into a bowl and mix on a slow to medium speed until combined. Leave the pastry in a refrigerator to chill for 30 min.
2 Roll out the pastry into a circle and line a 25cm (10in) flan dish. Ease the pastry into the dish, taking care not to stretch the dough. Trim off the excess pastry but leave 12mm (½in) above the edges of the dish. Tuck this under and press well into the sides. Flute or crimp the edges and prick the sides and base of the flan case well with a fork.
3 Using a long, smooth strip of aluminium foil, line the inside upright edge of the flan case. Place 2 pieces of kitchen paper over the base, easing around the edges and pressing gently into the corners to help keep the foil strip in position.
4 Cook, uncovered, in the microwave on 100% (full) setting for 6–7 min. Remove the paper and foil and cook for a further 1–1½ min. Leave to cool slightly.
5 Cut the brie into pieces and place into a bowl or dish. Cover and cook on 30% setting for about 6 min until the cheese is melted, stirring well 2–3 times throughout. Beat in the cream, milk, eggs, ginger, saffron with the water and a little salt to taste, until the mixture is smooth.
6 Pour the filling into the prepared flan case. Cover the flan with either a microwave plate cover or a suitable large dinner plate, and cook on 30% setting for 18–22 min until the filling is set and puffy. Turn the dish once during cooking.
7 Sprinkle the top of the tart with the demerara sugar or grated nutmeg if liked and place under a medium-hot grill for 5–10 min to glaze the surface. Serve straight away, garnished with cucumber.

DO NOT FREEZE

Savarin (page 104); Potato Salad with Parma Ham (page 17); Brie Tart (above); Chicken with Tomato Vinaigrette (page 16)

4 large tomatoes
salt and freshly ground black
    pepper
4 eggs
butter

for the sauce:
25g (1oz) butter
1 onion, finely chopped
25g (1oz) flour
½–1 × 15ml tbsp (½–1tbsp)
    curry powder
150ml (¼pt) chicken stock
    (page 20)
salt
150 (¼pt) single cream
50g (2oz) button mushrooms,
    sliced

Baked eggs with curry sauce (*serves 4*)
POWER LEVEL: 100% (FULL) AND 70%

1 Cut the tops from the tomatoes, remove the pulp and drain. Season the insides of the tomato cases with salt and a little black pepper.
2 Break an egg into each tomato case, prick the yolks and dot with butter. Season to taste and place on a plate. Cover with a lid or pierced clingfilm. Leave to one side while preparing the sauce.
3 Melt the butter in a bowl on 100% (full) setting for 1 min. Stir in the onion, cover and cook for 4 min. Mix in the flour and curry powder until blended then add the stock gradually.
4 Add a little salt and stir in the cream. Cook on 70% setting for about 8 min until thickened and blended. Stir in the sliced mushrooms and continue to cook for a further 4 min. Leave to stand.
5 Cook the eggs and tomatoes in the microwave for 4–5 min on 70% setting until the eggs are firm. Serve topped with the curry sauce.

DO NOT FREEZE

225g (8oz) cheddar, grated
2 courgettes *or* ½ cucumber,
    trimmed and grated
1 clove garlic, crushed
425ml (¾pt) natural yoghurt
1 × 15ml tbsp (1tbsp)
    mayonnaise (page 76)
½ × 5ml tsp (½tsp) mustard
    powder
1 × 15ml tbsp (1tbsp) chopped
    chives or parsley
½ × 5ml tsp (½tsp) paprika
salt and pepper
6 × 15ml tbsp (6tbsp) white
    wine or water
25g (1oz) *or* 2 packets gelatin
for garnish: paprika for
    sprinkling and watercress

Cheddar mousse (*serves 4–8*)
POWER LEVEL: 100% (FULL)

Serve either as a starter or a main course

1 In a large bowl mix together all the ingredients except the wine and gelatin.
2 Heat the wine in a small bowl or dish for 30 sec, add the gelatin and stir to dissolve. Heat for a further 15–30 sec, without boiling, and stir until the gelatin is completely dissolved. Beat the gelatin into the cheese mixture.
3 Rinse a 17·5cm (7in) ring mould in cold water. Spoon the mousse into the mould and smooth the top. Chill for several hours until set.
4 Ease the mousse away from the side of the mould with your fingertips and invert the mousse onto a serving plate. Sprinkle with a little paprika and garnish with watercress.

DO NOT FREEZE

25g (1oz) butter, approximately
2–3 × 15ml tbsp (2–3tbsp)
    brandy, port or wine,
    approximately
100–175g (4–6oz) left-over dry
    cheese
ground nutmeg, mace, paprika
    and black pepper to taste
50–75g (2–3oz) left-over stilton
    or blue cheese
one or more of the following
    additions to taste, optional:
    anchovy essence, tabasco
    sauce, crushed garlic,
    chopped parsley, chives,
    spring onion, dill, cumin,
    fennel, caraway, chopped
    nuts

Cheese in a pot (*serves 4–6*)
POWER LEVEL: 100% (FULL)

1 Heat the butter and brandy, port or wine for 1–2 min. Stir well and heat again until hot, about 1 min.
2 Add the dry cheese and seasonings to taste. Mix well together until blended. It may be necessary to heat again for 15–30 sec at a time until the cheese is softened. Be careful not to overheat otherwise the mixture may separate.
3 Crumble in the stilton or blue cheese and blend well. If preferred, the mixture may be blended in a liquidiser or food processor.
4 If the mixture seems a little dry, add more butter and/or brandy, port or wine until a smooth paste is made.
5 Add one or more of the alternative additions to taste. Pack into small pots and chill before serving.

Cook's note: *A wonderfully easy add-what-you-like recipe to use up those bits of stilton or left-over cheese. It is a useful alternative to a cheese board*

Spinach omelette *(serves 3–4)*
POWER LEVEL: 100% (FULL) AND 70%
CONVENTIONAL GRILL

This recipe is for a thick, unfolded omelette, served in wedges. The main ingredient, spinach, can be varied to include a mixture of spinach and sorrel or chard or grated courgettes

1 Trim and wash the fresh spinach thoroughly in several changes of cold water. Place in a large bowl with just the water clinging to the leaves, cover and cook for 8–10 min on 100% (full) setting, stirring 2–3 times throughout. Drain well, squeezing as much water from the leaves as possible. Roughly chop the spinach and add about 15g (½oz) butter.
2 If using frozen spinach, drain it thoroughly when thawed, add about 15g (½oz) butter and heat in the microwave on 100% (full) setting for 3–4 min until hot, stirring once or twice throughout.
3 Beat the eggs with seasoning and 25g (1oz) of the butter cut into slivers. If necessary, drain the spinach again and stir into the eggs. Add 25g (1oz) of butter to a 22·5–25cm (9–10in) round shallow dish and heat in the microwave for 1 min until the butter is melted. Swirl the butter around to coat the base and side of the dish.
4 Pour the egg and spinach mixture into the dish and smooth the top. Cover and cook on 70% setting for 8–10 min, stirring after 1½–2 min to bring the edges of the omelette into the centre.
5 Sprinkle with the grated cheese and brown the top under a hot grill. Alternatively, cook uncovered in the microwave on 100% (full) setting for 2–3 min to melt the cheese.

DO NOT FREEZE

900g (2lb) fresh spinach *or* 675g (1½lb) frozen spinach, thawed
65g (2½oz) butter
6 eggs, size 3, beaten
salt and freshly ground black pepper
75g (3oz) cheese, grated, eg parmesan, cheddar, double gloucester, to choice

Cheese pizza casserole *(serves 6–8)*
POWER LEVEL: 60%

The ingredients are layered into a gratin dish and the assembled dish is then baked in the microwave before being browned under a hot grill or in a preheated oven

1 Pour the milk into a shallow dish and dip in 5 of the bread slices to moisten them. Arrange the slices attractively in the base of a 25–30cm (10–12in) round, deep gratin dish which has been lightly buttered.
2 Coat the bread with a layer of tomato sauce then sprinkle with a little of the oregano. Cover with a layer of mozzarella cheese.
3 Reserving 4–5 × 15ml tbsp (4–5tbsp) of the sauce and about 65–75g (2½–3oz) of the mozzarella, continue the layers in the dish. Dip the bread slices in the milk as you go and finish with a layer of bread. Press the layers down firmly with a spatula.
4 Beat the eggs with the parmesan cheese and add a little seasoning to taste. Pour the mixture over the layers, ensuring the top bread layer is thoroughly coated.
5 Allow the dish to stand for 5 min, piercing through the layers with a skewer if necessary to let the egg mixture penetrate through to the bottom layers.
6 Arrange the reserved mozzarella slices and spoonfuls of tomato sauce attractively on the top and dot with the slivers of butter.
7 Cover the dish with a lid or pierced clingfilm and cook on 60% setting for 30–35 min, turning the dish once or twice throughout if necessary.
8 Brown the top of the pizza casserole under a medium-hot grill or place in a preheated hot oven for 15–20 min.

DO NOT FREEZE

425–550ml (¾–1pt) milk
20 thin slices bread
550ml (1pt) tomato sauce (page 74)
1–2 × 15ml tbsp (1–2tbsp) chopped fresh oregano *or* 1–2 × 5ml tsp (1–2tsp) dried oregano
550–675g (1¼–1½lb) mozzarella cheese, thinly sliced
6 eggs
4–5 × 15ml tbsp (4–5tbsp) grated parmesan cheese
salt and freshly ground black pepper
slivers of butter

450g (1lb) shelled peas
3 × 15ml tbsp (3tbsp) salted
    water
salt and freshly ground black
    pepper
large knob of butter
150ml (¼pt) double cream
4 eggs

Eggs en cocotte with purée of peas (serves 4)   *colour opposite*
POWER LEVEL: 100% (FULL) AND 70%

1 Cook the peas with the salted water in a covered container for 10–12 min until tender, stirring the peas or shaking the dish twice throughout.
2 Drain the peas and rub them through a sieve or purée them in a food processor or blender, or sieve them to remove any pieces of skin.
3 Add salt and pepper to taste, beat in the butter and about half of the cream. Turn the purée into an oval gratin dish or individual serving dishes. Smooth the surface with a spoon or spatula then hollow out 4 oval or round shapes to hold the eggs.
4 Break each egg into a hollow, pierce the yolks and sprinkle with salt and pepper. Spoon the remaining cream over the eggs. Cover the dish with pierced clingfilm or a lid and cook for 8–10 min on 70% setting until the eggs are set, rearranging the dish if necessary halfway through.
5 Allow to stand for 3–4 min and serve onto hot serving dishes.

DO NOT FREEZE

Cook's note: *A purée of cooked mushrooms or spinach could be used instead. Allow 6–8 min on 70% setting if 4 individual servings are being cooked together, and give extra time if required.*

350g (12oz) courgettes, grated
salt
150–275ml (¼–½pt) tomato
    sauce (page 74)
1 red pepper, deseeded
50–75g (2–3oz) butter
75–100g (3–4oz) cheddar
    cheese, grated
6 eggs, size 3
freshly ground black pepper
75ml (2½fl oz) double cream
25–50g (1–2oz) browned
    breadcrumbs

Courgette omelettes au gratin (serves 3–4)   *colour opposite*
POWER LEVEL: 100% (FULL)
CONVENTIONAL GRILL

The microwave cooker can produce deliciously light omelettes but of course without the traditional browning. In this recipe several omelettes are cooked and then combined with a selection of other ingredients which can be varied to choice. The complete assembled dish is then browned under a hot grill

1 Place the grated courgettes into a colander, sprinkle liberally with salt and cover with a plate. Leave for 30 min to degorge.
2 Meanwhile, strain the tomato sauce or purée in a food processor or blender if preferred. Reheat for 2–3 min if necessary and keep warm.
3 Cut the red pepper into quarters lengthways and brown the skins under a hot grill. Peel off and disgard the skins and cut the flesh into thin strips.
4 Rinse and drain the courgettes. Add a knob of butter and cook, uncovered, for 3 min.
5 Lightly butter an oval, heatproof gratin dish and sprinkle with some of the cheese.
6 Beat the eggs in a measuring jug with salt and pepper and the cream. Stir the courgettes into the eggs.
7 Add a small knob of butter to a 15–17·5cm (6–7in) round, shallow dish. Heat the butter for 30–60 sec and swirl it around to coat all the dish.
8 Add a quarter of the egg and courgette mixture. Cook, uncovered, for about 20–30 sec and then stir, bringing the edges of the omelette towards the centre of the dish. Cover with a lid and continue to cook for a further 1¼–1½ min until the omelette is set but still moist.
9 Using a spatula, ease the omelette away from the dish and slide it unfolded into the prepared gratin dish. Cover and keep warm. Make 3 more omelettes in the same way and arrange them overlapping in the dish.
10 Sprinkle the omelettes with a little more cheese, and arrange the strips of pepper over the top. Spoon over the tomato sauce and finally sprinkle with the remaining cheese mixed with the breadcrumbs.
11 Place the dish under a medium-hot grill to melt the cheese and brown the surface. Serve straight away from the gratin dish.

Egg en Cocotte with Purée of Peas (above); Courgette Omlettes au Gratin (above)

DO NOT FREEZE

50g (2oz) butter
225g (8oz) cream cheese
1 egg yolk
1–2 cloves garlic, crushed
salt
2 × 15ml tbsp (2tbsp) fresh
  chopped herbs to choice *or*
  1 × 15ml tbsp (1 tbsp) dried
  herbs
for serving: toasted bread cases
  (below), optional, or fingers
  of toast

Cheese and herb pâté *(serves 4)*
POWER LEVEL: 50%

1 Place the butter in a bowl or dish and melt it in the microwave on 50% setting for about 3½–4 min. Leave to cool.
2 Beat together the cheese, egg yolk, garlic and a little salt. Fold in the herbs and add the cooled butter, then leave to chill.
3 Use straight away, spooned into the toasted bread cases, or serve with fingers of toast.

Cook's note: *This mixture may be piped into swirls and frozen for use another time or can be used to decorate savoury dishes*

6 large slices bread, cut 2·5cm
  (1in) thick
50–75g (2–3oz) butter

Toasted bread cases *(makes 6)*
POWER LEVEL: 100% (FULL)
CONVENTIONAL OVEN TEMPERATURE: 180°C (350°F) MARK 4

1 Cut rounds from the bread slices using a 9–10cm (3½–4in) cutter. Cut a circle inside the round using a cutter 12mm (½in) smaller, cutting down to within about 1cm (⅓in) of the base.
2 Insert a knife into the side of the bread round at 1cm (⅓cm) above the base, and cutting horizontally and swivelling the knife, cut away the centre section.
3 Melt the butter for 2–2½ min and brush the bread cases inside and out with the melted butter.
4 Bake in a preheated oven for about 20 min until golden brown.

Cook's note: *Alternatively, sprinkle the cases with a little paprika, place onto kitchen paper towel and cook in the microwave for 5–6 min, although not such a crisp result will be obtained*

Individual pastry flan cases *(makes 6–8)*
POWER LEVEL: 100% (FULL) OR
CONVENTIONAL OVEN TEMPERATURE: 220°C (425°F) MARK 7

Follow the ingredients for the flan pastry case for brie tart on page 58 which is sufficient to line six to eight 10–12·5cm (4–5in) individual microwave flan dishes or flan tins. Trim the edges and prick the sides and bases well with a fork. Place in a circle on the microwave cooker shelf and cook for 5–7 min, rearranging the dishes half-way through if necessary. Alternatively place the tins onto baking trays and bake conventionally in a pre-heated oven for 15–20 min until golden brown.

Dressed vegetables

Potato soufflés (serves 4)
POWER LEVEL: 100% (FULL)
CONVENTIONAL OVEN TEMPERATURE: 200°C (400°F) MARK 6

4 large potatoes, scrubbed
40g (1½oz) butter
85ml (3fl oz) double cream
2 eggs, separated
salt and pepper

1 Prick the potato skins with a fork. Weigh them and then cook, uncovered, in the microwave allowing 10–12 min per ½kg (1lb). Turn the potatoes over halfway through.
2 Cut a slice lengthways from each potato carefully and scoop out the insides leaving a thin shell. Mash the soft potato well with the butter, double cream, egg yolks and seasoning to taste. Alternatively purée in a blender or food processor.
3 Beat the egg whites until stiff with a little salt and fold into the potato mixture. Pile the filling back into the potato shells and place on a baking tray. Cook in the preheated oven for 15–20 min until the soufflés are well risen and browned.
4 Serve straight away before the soufflés have time to collapse.

DO NOT FREEZE

Chou-fleur polonais (serves 4–6)   colour page 43
POWER LEVEL: 100% (FULL)

1 cauliflower, weighing about 675g (1½lb)
4 × 15ml tbsp (4tbsp) salted water
1 hard-boiled egg
25g (1oz) butter
25g (1oz) dried breadcrumbs
2 × 15ml tbsp (2tbsp) chopped parsley
salt and freshly ground black pepper
squeeze lemon juice

1 Trim the cauliflower and place in a bowl or dish with the salted water. Cover and cook for 10–11 min, allow to stand for 3 min.
2 Meanwhile, remove the egg whites from the yolks, chop the whites finely with a sharp stainless-steel knife and sieve the yolks.
3 Melt the butter in a shallow dish for 1 min, stir in the breadcrumbs and cook, uncovered, for 2–2½ min, tossing over well halfway through. If preferred, the breadcrumbs may be lightly fried in the butter in a frypan until golden brown.
4 Stir in the parsley, seasoning and lemon juice. Drain the cauliflower and place onto a hot serving dish. Spoon over the breadcrumb mixture, gently pressing it onto the surface, and decorate attractively with the chopped egg white and sieved egg yolk. Serve hot.

DO NOT FREEZE

Cook's note: *You need patience to decorate the top of the cauliflower with the egg yolk and white but, if time permits, the effect is well worthwhile. Otherwise, mix the two together and sprinkle over the breadcrumbs*

Brussels sprouts with chestnuts (serves 6–8)   colour page 67
POWER LEVEL: 100% (FULL) AND 50%

225g (8oz) dried chestnuts
boiling water
boiling chicken or vegetable stock (page 20)
675g (1½lb) brussels sprouts, trimmed and washed
4 × 15ml tbsp (4tbsp) salted water
40g (1½oz) butter
salt and freshly ground black pepper

A traditional Christmas lunch vegetable dish to serve with poultry or game, but using dried chestnuts for convenience

1 Place the dried chestnuts in a bowl and pour on sufficient boiling water to cover. Cover the dish with a lid or pierced clingfilm and cook on 100% (full) setting for 5 min. Allow to stand for 1 hr and then drain.
2 Pour sufficient stock over the soaked chestnuts to cover them. Cover the dish and cook on 50% setting for 20–25 min until tender. Leave to stand while the sprouts are cooking.

3   Place the sprouts in a suitable container or boiling bag with the salted water and cook on 100% (full) setting for 11–13 min, stirring once throughout. Drain the sprouts and the chestnuts.
4   Melt the butter for 1–1½ min on 100% (full) setting, add the sprouts and chestnuts with seasoning to taste and mix well together. Transfer to a hot vegetable dish and serve.

Cook's note: *If fresh chestnuts are preferred, skin them by slitting the skins with a sharp knife and then heating 10–12 at a time in the microwave on 100% (full) setting until hot, about 1–1½ min. Peel off the skins while hot and then cook in the stock as above*

900g (2lb) jerusalem artichokes
150ml (¼pt) milk and water mixed
40g (1½oz) butter
1 onion, finely chopped
175g (6oz) flat mushrooms, finely chopped
25g (1oz) flour
150ml (¼pt) chicken or veal stock (page 20), approximately
salt and pepper
1 bay leaf
1 × 15ml tbsp (1tbsp) chopped mint or parsley

Artichokes duxelles *(serves 6–8)*   *colour opposite*
POWER LEVEL: 100% (FULL)

1   Peel the artichokes and cut into even-sized pieces. Place into a large bowl with the milk and water. Cover and cook for 18–20 min until just tender, stirring 2–3 times throughout, and leave to stand.
2   Melt the butter in a large bowl or dish for 1–1½ min, add the onion, cover and cook for 5 min. Stir in the mushrooms and cook, uncovered, for 2 min. Stir in the flour.
3   Drain the artichokes and reserve the liquid. Make up to 275ml (½pt) with the stock. Add this to the sauce gradually and mix well together. Add salt and pepper to taste and the bay leaf.
4   Cook for 3–4 until thickened and boiling, stirring every minute. Place the artichokes into a hot serving dish. Remove the bay leaf from the sauce and adjust the seasoning.
5   Spoon the sauce over the artichokes and reheat, covered, for 2 min. Sprinkle with the chopped mint or parsley before serving.

4–5 medium-sized aubergines
salt
150–200ml (5–7fl oz) olive oil
1–2 cloves garlic, crushed
1 onion, finely chopped
450g (1lb) ripe tomatoes, skinned, deseeded and chopped *or* 400g (14oz) can chopped tomatoes
1 × 15ml tbsp (1tbsp) tomato purée
salt and pepper
150ml (¼pt) natural yoghurt
4 × 15ml tbsp (4tbsp) stock (page 20)
for garnish: chopped parsley, optional

Aubergine galette *(serves 6–8)*   *colour opposite*
POWER LEVEL: 100% (FULL) AND 30%

1   Wipe the aubergines and cut into thin slices diagonally. Sprinkle with salt and leave to degorge for 30 min.
2   Meanwhile, place 2 × 15ml tbsp (2tbsp) of the oil in a bowl, stir in the garlic and onion, cover and cook for 3 min on 100% (full) setting. Add the tomatoes, tomato purée and seasoning and continue to cook, uncovered, for 8–10 min until thick.
3   Rinse and drain the aubergine slices and pat dry. Place them in a large bowl or dish with sufficient oil to coat the slices lightly.
4   Cover and cook on 100% (full) setting for 8–10 min until just tender, stirring well or shaking the dish 2–3 times throughout. Leave to cool slightly.
5   Using two-thirds of the tomato mixture, layer with the aubergine slices and spoonfuls of yoghurt in a 17·5–20cm (7–8in) round, deep dish, beginning and ending with a layer of aubergines. Press the layers down lightly.
6   Cover and cook on 30% setting for 35–40 min. Allow to stand for 3 min before turning out onto a hot serving dish. Heat the rest of the tomato sauce with the stock for 2–3 min on 100% (full) setting and pour over the galette. Serve garnished with a little chopped parsley if required.

Brussels Sprouts with Chestnuts (page 65); Artichokes Duxelles (above); Aubergine Galette (above)

DO NOT FREEZE

50–75g (2–3oz) butter
1 onion, chopped
1 white cabbage, weighing
    about 900g (2lb)
215ml (7½fl oz) soured cream
salt and freshly ground black
    pepper
½ × 5ml tsp (½tsp) paprika
squeeze lemon juice

Austrian cabbage *(serves 6–8)*
POWER LEVEL: 100% (FULL) AND 30%

1 Melt 50g (2oz) of the butter in a large bowl for 1½ min on 100% (full) setting. Add the chopped onion, cover and cook for 3 min.
2 Remove the outer leaves of the cabbage, cut into quarters and cut out the stalks. Shred the cabbage leaves finely and stir into the bowl with the onion. Toss well in the butter and add a little more butter if necessary to ensure the cabbage is well coated.
3 Cover and cook on 100% (full) setting for 10 min, stirring twice during cooking. Stir in 150ml (5fl oz) of the soured cream and season to taste with salt, pepper and paprika.
4 Cover and cook on 30% setting for 30–45 min until the cabbage is tender, stirring 2–3 times throughout. Add the remaining soured cream and a squeeze of lemon juice to taste. Adjust the seasoning and serve straight away.

DO NOT FREEZE

6 large firm tomatoes
40g (1½oz) butter
1 small onion, finely chopped
275ml (½pt) cooked peas
2 × 5ml tsp (2tsp) chopped
    mint
salt and freshly ground black
    pepper
1 egg yolk
for garnish: 6 black olives

Tomatoes with purée of green peas *(serves 6)*
POWER LEVEL: 100% (FULL)

1 Cut a slice from the tops of the tomatoes and reserve. Scoop out the core and seeds with a teaspoon and discard. Turn the tomato cups upside down to drain.
2 Melt the butter in a bowl for 1–1½ min, stir in the onion, cover and cook for 3 min until tender. Stir in the peas, mint and seasoning to taste. Cover and cook for 2–3 min until heated through.
3 Place the onion and pea mixture into a food processor or blender and purée, or rub the mixture through a sieve. Beat in the egg yolk and cook in the microwave for 30–60 sec until the mixture thickens, stirring every 30 sec. Do not allow to boil. Set the mixture to one side to cool and thicken.
4 Sprinkle the insides of the tomatoes with salt and pepper and spoon in the puréed filling. Replace the tomato lids and secure with a wooden cocktail stick.
5 Arrange the tomatoes in a circle on a plate or in a casserole dish and cover with a lid or clingfilm. Cook for 4–5 min until heated through. Garnish with an olive on the top of each cocktail stick and serve hot.

Calabrese with poulette sauce *(serves 4–6)*   *colour page 11*
POWER LEVEL: 100% (FULL)

Calabrese or green broccoli contrasts well with the classic creamy white sauce. Serve as a starter or as a special vegetable dish with the main course

1 Place the broccoli in a casserole dish with the curds towards the centre of the dish. Add the salted water, cover and cook for 10–14 min, stirring once during cooking. The cooking time will vary with the size of the broccoli heads. Allow to stand for a few minutes while preparing the sauce.
2 Melt the butter for 1–2 min, stir in the flour and blend well together. Drain the broccoli and stir the cooking liquid into the roux. Heat for 2–3 min until thickened, stirring every 30 sec, and beat well.
3 Beat the egg yolk with the lemon juice and some of the hot sauce. Blend well together and add to the rest of the sauce, beating well. Stir in 3 × 15ml tbsp (3tbsp) of the cream and heat for 15–30 sec but do not allow the sauce to boil. Add a little more cream if necessary to achieve a thick batter consistency.
4 Place the drained broccoli into a hot serving dish. Adjust the seasoning of the sauce and spoon it over the broccoli. Serve straight away.

DO NOT FREEZE

675g (1½lb) green broccoli, washed and trimmed
4 × 15ml tbsp (4tbsp) salted water

for the sauce:
50g (2oz) butter
2 × 5ml tsp (2tsp) flour
1 egg yolk
juice ½ lemon
3–5 × 15ml tbsp (3–5tbsp) double cream
salt and freshly ground black pepper

Courgettes gratinées *(serves 4)*
POWER LEVEL: 100% (FULL) AND 70%

1 Cut the courgettes into 6mm (¼in) slices, cutting diagonally across each courgette. Place into a dish or bowl with a tight-fitting lid or use clingfilm.
2 Cook for 8–10 min on 100% (full) setting until tender, shaking the dish or stirring once throughout. Drain, then sprinkle with salt and pepper to taste.
3 Beat together lightly the egg, cream and 2 × 15ml tbsp (2tbsp) of the cheese. Season with a little black pepper.
4 Place the courgettes into a shallow serving dish and pour over the egg and cream mixture. Sprinkle with the remaining cheese and top with slivers of butter.
5 Cook, uncovered, on 70% setting for about 4–5 min until set and heated through. Sprinkle with paprika before serving or alternatively brown the top under a medium-hot grill.

DO NOT FREEZE

450g (1lb) courgettes, washed or wiped and trimmed
salt and freshly ground black pepper
1 egg, beaten
75ml (2½fl oz) double cream
3 × 15ml tbsp (3tbsp) grated gruyère cheese
slivers butter
for garnish: paprika for sprinkling, optional

Champignons à la crème *(serves 4)*
POWER LEVEL: 100% (FULL)

1 Melt the butter for 1–1½ min in a bowl or dish. Add the mushrooms and toss them over well in the butter. Cook, uncovered, for 2½–3 min, stirring once during cooking.
2 Add the salt and freshly ground black pepper and the mixed herbs and continue to cook for a further 2–3 min.
3 Sprinkle the flour into the dish and mix well to blend the ingredients. Stir in the double cream gradually and cook in the microwave for 1½–2 min, until thickened, stirring every 30 sec.
4 Stir in the lemon juice and parsley, reheat if necessary for 30 sec and serve straight away.

40g (1½oz) butter
450g (1lb) button mushrooms, wiped and trimmed
salt and freshly ground black pepper
2 × 5ml tsp (2tsp) chopped fresh mixed herbs
1 × 15ml tbsp (1tbsp) flour
150ml (¼pt) double cream
juice ½ lemon
1 × 15ml tbsp (1tbsp) chopped parsley

25g (1oz) butter
2 × 15ml tbsp (2tbsp) olive oil
4 large red or green peppers,
    deseeded and cut into thin
    strips
1 onion, finely chopped
8 tomatoes, skinned and
    roughly chopped
1–2 cloves garlic, crushed
salt and freshly ground black
    pepper
1–2 × 5ml tsp (1–2tsp) caster
    sugar to taste

1 clove garlic
15g (½oz) butter
450g (1lb) waxy potatoes,
    peeled
salt and freshly ground black
    pepper
275ml (½pt) double cream
slivers butter

Peperonata (serves 4–6)   *colour opposite*
POWER LEVEL: 100% (FULL)

This dish of peppers and tomatoes originates from Italy and can be served with plain roast or grilled meats, or as a starter or side salad

1 Heat the butter and oil in a large casserole dish for 1½–2 min. Add the peppers and onion, cover and cook for 6–8 min until the vegetables are tender, stirring 2–3 times throughout cooking.
2 Add the tomatoes, garlic, seasoning and sugar to taste. Cook, uncovered, for a further 5–6 min when the mixture should be quite soft and the juices slightly evaporated.
3 Sprinkle with a little freshly ground black pepper and serve hot with grilled or roast meat, or fish, or cold as a starter or side salad.

Gratin dauphinois (serves 2–4)
POWER LEVEL: 100% (FULL) AND 70%
CONVENTIONAL GRILL

An excellent potato dish to serve with plain meats but it is also delicious enough to serve on its own as a starter or vegetable course.
To quote Elizabeth David: 'If it seems to the thrifty minded outrageously extravagant to use half a pint of cream to one pound of potatoes, I can only say that to me it seems a more satisfactory way of enjoying cream than pouring it over tinned peaches or chocolate mousse'

1 Rub the cut edge of the clove of garlic well around the inside of a 17·5–20cm (7–8in) shallow, round, heatproof gratin dish. Add the butter and heat for 30 sec on 100% (full) setting. Brush the butter around the sides of the dish.
2 Cut the potatoes into very thin slices. This is easier if using a mandoline or food processor, or slicer attachment for a food mixer. Rinse the slices well and dry.
3 Layer the potato slices in the dish, sprinkling each layer with salt and pepper. Finally pour on the cream and top with slivers of butter.
4 Reduce to 70% setting and cook, covered, for about 20–25 min. Stand for 5 min before browning the top slowly under a medium-hot grill to glaze and crust the surface.

DO NOT FREEZE

Almondine potatoes (serves 3–4)
POWER LEVEL: 100% (FULL)

Follow the methods and ingredients for creamed potatoes (page 72), omitting the milk but stirring in the butter, seasonings and a little cream. Allow the mixture to cool sufficiently to handle and divide into 8–10 small balls, shaping between the palms of the hands and using a little flour if necessary to prevent sticking. Roll the potato balls in a little egg white and then into finely chopped and toasted almonds. Place onto a serving plate or dish and heat through for about 3 min until hot.

Almond croquettes   *colour page 15*

Follow the above recipe but instead of using chopped toasted almonds, roll the potatoes in flaked almonds. Heat a pan of oil or lard to a temperature of about 180°C (350°F) and fry the croquettes until golden brown. Drain on kitchen paper towel before serving hot.

Peperonata (above); Pistachio and Raisin Pilaff (page 81); Poulet à la Suisse (page 53)

Creamed potatoes *(serves 4–6)*
POWER LEVEL: 100% (FULL)

Boil about 1¼kg (2½lb) peeled potatoes which have been cut into even size small pieces, in a covered container with 6 × 15ml tbsp (6tbsp) salted water for about 20 min. Toss over or stir the potatoes well 3–4 times during cooking. Drain and mash with a fork or potato masher. Beat in a knob of butter and add up to 150ml (¼pt) hot milk. Add salt and pepper and little cream to taste.

2 heads of fennel, washed and
    trimmed
75g (3oz) butter
salt and freshly ground black
    pepper
1 lemon, grated rind and juice
2 × 15ml tbsp (2tbsp) chopped
    fresh mixed herbs

Sauté of fennel *(serves 4–6)*
POWER LEVEL: 100% (FULL)

1   Cut the fennel into 6mm (¼in) slices. Place half the butter in a large bowl or dish and heat for 1–1½ min until melted. Add the fennel slices and toss well in the butter. Add salt and pepper to taste and mix well.
2   Cover the dish with a lid or pierced clingfilm and cook for about 12 min, shaking the dish or stirring twice throughout. Remove the lid or clingfilm from the dish and cook, uncovered, for 2–3 min to evaporate some of the liquid. Place the fennel into a hot serving dish and keep warm.
3   Add the rest of the butter to the cooking dish and heat in the microwave until it bubbles and begins to foam. Add the lemon rind and juice and the herbs. Pour over the fennel and serve hot.

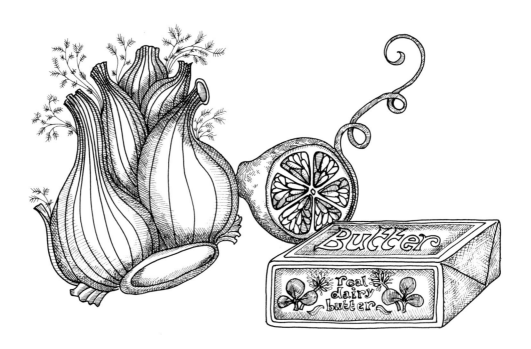

Sauces

Soured cream and mushroom sauce *(makes about 275ml/1/2pt)*
POWER LEVEL: 100% (FULL) AND 50%

1 Melt the butter for 1 min on 100% (full) setting. Add the mushrooms, toss well in the butter and cook, uncovered, for 1½ min.
2 Stir in the flour and continue to cook for a further 30 sec. Stir in the wine or sherry gradually, until smooth and well blended, the white stock and soured cream. Add salt and pepper to taste.
3 Cook on 50% setting for about 8 min until thickened, stirring well 2–3 times throughout. Be careful not to let the sauce boil.
4 Adjust the seasoning and serve with roast meat, grills and game.

DO NOT FREEZE

25g (1oz) butter
100g (4oz) mushrooms, sliced
25g (1oz) flour
4 × 15ml tbsp (4tbsp) dry white wine or sherry
150ml (¼pt) white stock (page 20)
150ml (¼pt) soured cream
salt and freshly ground black pepper

Espagnole (basic brown) sauce *(makes about 1 litre/1¾pt)*
POWER LEVEL: 100% (FULL) AND 50%

1 Melt the butter for 1 min in a covered bowl or casserole dish. Stir in the carrot, onion and celery, cover and cook for 5–6 min on 100% (full) setting, stirring halfway through.
2 Add the bacon and mushrooms and continue to cook, uncovered, for 3 min. Stir in the flour and cook for 30 sec.
3 Stir in the hot stock gradually until well blended and add the tomato purée, bay leaf and parsley. Cover and cook for 4–5 min until thickened and boiling, stirring once or twice throughout.
4 Reduce to 50% setting and continue to cook uncovered for 30–40 min until the vegetables are tender and the sauce is well flavoured.
5 Strain the sauce, pressing the juices from the vegetables etc to extract as much flavour from them as possible. Add the sherry (only if serving as the basic sauce) and seasoning. Serve with red meats and game.

40g (1½oz) butter
1 carrot, finely chopped
1 onion, finely chopped
½ stick celery, finely chopped
40g (1½oz) lean bacon, cut into shreds
75–100g (3–4oz) mushrooms, finely chopped
2 × 15ml tbsp (2tbsp) flour
1 litre (1¾pt) hot brown stock (page 20)
2–3 × 5ml tsp (2–3tsp) tomato purée
1 bay leaf
3 sprigs parsley
75ml (2½fl oz) brown sherry, optional
salt and freshly ground black pepper

Variations

Sauce bordelaise
Add 100ml (4fl oz) red wine and 1 finely chopped shallot to a scant 550ml (1pt) espagnole sauce. Heat on 100% (full) setting until boiling then cook, uncovered, on 70% setting until reduced by about half. Stir in 1–2 × 15ml tbsp (1–2tbsp) finely chopped parsley and adjust the seasoning. Serve with roast beef, tournedos and dark game.

Sauce chasseur
Cook 1 finely chopped shallot and 75g (3oz) chopped mushrooms in 15g (½oz) butter for 4 min on 100% (full) setting. Add 150ml (¼pt) white wine and cook, uncovered, until it has reduced by half. Stir in 275ml (½pt) espagnole sauce and 2 × 5ml tsp (2tsp) tomato purée. Add a little chopped parsley before serving. Serve with various meats, rabbit and chicken dishes.

Sauce demi-glace
Cook 1–2 chopped mushrooms or mushroom peelings and stems in 6 × 15ml tbsp (6tbsp) dry sherry or madeira on 100% (full) setting, uncovered, until the liquid is reduced by half. Cook 425ml (¾pt) espagnole sauce, uncovered, until reduced by a third. Add 1–2 × 15ml tbsp (1–2tbsp) meat glaze and the reduced sherry to the sauce and cook for 10 min on 50% setting. Strain before serving with meats.

1 × 15ml tbsp (1tbsp) olive oil
1 large onion, finely chopped
1–2 cloves garlic, crushed
675g (1½lb) tomatoes, skinned
    or 1 × 400g (14oz) can
    tomatoes
1–2 × 15ml tbsp (1–2tbsp)
    tomato purée
1 wine glass red wine
few sprigs fresh herbs
salt and freshly ground black
    pepper
1–2 × 15ml tbsp (1–2tbsp)
    chopped fresh oregano or
    basil

Tomato sauce *(makes about 275ml/¹/2pt)*
POWER LEVEL: 100% (FULL)

1 Place the olive oil, onion and garlic into a bowl and stir well. Cover and cook for 4–5 min until soft.
2 Roughly chop the tomatoes and add to the dish with the remaining ingredients. Cook, uncovered, until soft and the liquid quantity is reduced, giving a fairly thick sauce. Stir 2–3 times during cooking.

1 small onion
6 cloves
1 bay leaf
6 peppercorns
1 blade mace
275ml (½pt) milk
25g (1oz) butter
25g (1oz) flour
salt and white pepper

Béchamel sauce *(makes about 275ml/¹/2pt)*
POWER LEVEL: 50% AND 100% (FULL)

1 Peel the onion and stick with the cloves. Place into a bowl with the remaining spices and the milk. Heat on 50% setting for 10–11 min to allow the infusion of the flavours from the spices into the milk.
2 Melt the butter for 1 min on 100% (full) setting and stir in the flour and seasoning. Strain the milk and add a little at a time to the roux, stirring continuously.
3 Cook for 1½–2 min on 100% (full) until the sauce has thickened and is boiling, stirring or whisking frequently throughout. Adjust seasoning to taste. Serve with vegetables or combine with poultry or meats for croquettes or mousses.

Variations

Anchovy sauce   *colour opposite*
Stir 1–2 × 15ml tbsp (1–2tbsp) anchovy essence and a little lemon juice into the sauce. Serve with eggs and fish.

Aurore sauce
Stir 1–1½ × 15ml tbsp (1–1½tbsp) tomato purée and a knob of butter into the sauce. Serve with chicken, eggs or fish.

Cream sauce
Stir 75ml (2½fl oz) fresh cream and a few drops of lemon juice into the sauce. Serve with poultry, fish, eggs or vegetables.

Egg sauce
Stir 1 chopped hard-boiled egg and a little chopped parsley or chives into the sauce. Serve with poultry, fish or vegetables.

Herb sauce
Stir 1–1½ × 15ml tbsp (1–1½tbsp) freshly chopped tarragon, dill or parsley or other herbs to choice into the sauce. Serve with fish or poultry.

Mornay sauce
Stir 50g (2oz) mixed grated parmesan and gruyère cheeses and a little french mustard into the sauce. Beat until blended and reheat for 30 sec if necessary. Serve with fish, eggs, vegetables or pasta dishes.

Soubise sauce
Add 2–3 × 15ml tbsp (2–3tbsp) onion purée to the sauce and cook for 3 min on 50% setting, stirring twice throughout. Strain the sauce if preferred and add 150ml (¼pt) cream. Serve with fish, lamb, veal or sweetbreads.

Poached Egg with Anchovy Sauce
(page 57 and above)

40g (1½oz) butter
40g (1½oz) flour
550ml (1pt) hot white stock
    (page 20)
1–2 × 5ml tsp (1–2tsp) finely
    chopped parsley or dill or
    grated horseradish, optional

Velouté sauce *(makes about 550ml/1pt)*
POWER LEVEL: 100% (FULL) AND 50%

1 Melt the butter for 1 min in a bowl. Stir in the flour and add the stock gradually until well blended and smooth.
2 Heat until boiling on 100% (full) setting, stirring every minute, and then reduce to 50% setting and cook for 10 min uncovered. Whisk well occasionally during cooking.
3 Serve the sauce as it is or add finely chopped parsley, dill or grated horseradish. Serve with veal, chicken or lamb.

Onion sauce
Cook a small chopped onion on 100% (full) setting for 2 min in the butter before making the basic velouté sauce. Season to taste with wine vinegar and sugar. Serve with beef dishes.

2 egg yolks
salt and freshly ground black
    pepper
½ × 5ml tsp (½tsp) dijon
    mustard
lemon juice
275ml (½pt) olive oil

Mayonnaise *(makes about 275ml/½pt)*

1 Place the egg yolks, seasoning and mustard into a small bowl and mix well together. Add a little lemon juice.
2 Stir in the oil, drop by drop at first, and slowly increase the quantity, adding a little more lemon juice to taste until it is thick and smooth.
3 Correct the seasoning. Serve with salads.

DO NOT FREEZE

Variations
Blender mayonnaise
Blend the egg yolks (a whole egg may be used if preferred), seasoning, mustard and lemon juice in a food processor or blender. While the blade is still running, pour in the oil slowly through the hole in the lid until thick.

Lemon mayonnaise
Omit the mustard from the mayonnaise and add extra lemon juice to taste. Serve with fish, asparagus and shellfish.

Aïoli
Make a thick mayonnaise with crushed garlic to taste. Serve with meats, salads, fish and new potatoes in their jackets.

Sauce tartare
Make a mayonnaise with white vinegar instead of lemon juice and add 1 × 5ml tsp (1tsp) each of finely chopped capers, gherkins, parsley, tarragon and chervil. Stir in a pinch of sugar to taste. Serve with fried fish and shellfish.

Sauce rémoulade
Add 1 × 15ml tbsp (1tbsp) each finely chopped tarragon, basil and parsley, 1 × 5ml tsp (1tsp) each of finely chopped capers and gherkins, 2 × 5ml tsp (2tsp) mixed english and french mustard and a little anchovy essence to taste. Serve with grilled fish, prawns, lobster or cold pork.

Sauce verte
Place a handful of parsley, 3–4 sprigs each of tarragon and chervil, and a handful of washed spinach into a bowl with 2 × 15ml tbsp (2tbsp) water. Cover and cook for 3–4 min on 100% (full) setting until just tender. Drain, press and rub through a sieve or purée in a blender. Just before serving, add the purée to 275ml (½pt) mayonnaise and stir in 1–2 × 15ml tbsp (1–2tbsp) cream. Serve with salmon, salmon trout and other cold fish.

Béarnaise sauce *(makes about 150ml/¼pt)*
POWER LEVEL: 100% (FULL) AND 50%

1 Place the vinegar, peppercorns, bay leaf, tarragon and chervil sprigs and shallot into a small bowl. Cook, uncovered, on 100% (full) setting for 4–5 min until reduced to about a tablespoon.
2 Cream the egg yolks with 15g (½oz) butter and a pinch of salt. Strain the vinegar onto the eggs.
3 Whisk in the remaining butter, a small knob at a time, until the sauce is shiny. Heat on 50% setting for 15 sec at a time until the sauce is light and thickened.
4 Season to taste and stir in the chopped herbs. Serve with steaks, tournedos and grills.

DO NOT FREEZE

4 × 15ml tbsp (4tbsp) white wine vinegar
6 peppercorns
1 bay leaf
1 sprig each of tarragon and chervil
1 small shallot, finely chopped
2 egg yolks
salt and white pepper
90g (3½oz) butter, softened
1 × 5ml tsp (1tsp) each of finely chopped tarragon and chervil

Sauce choron
Make a béarnaise sauce as above and flavour to taste with tomato purée. Serve with chicken, fish and eggs.

Hollandaise sauce *(makes about 175ml/6fl oz)*
POWER LEVEL: 100% (FULL) AND 50%

1 Place the water and vinegar or wine into a bowl and cook, uncovered, on 100% (full) setting for about 4 min until reduced to about a tablespoon. Leave to cool.
2 Cream together the egg yolks, 15g (½oz) of the butter and a pinch of salt. Add the vinegar onto the eggs.
3 Whisk in the remaining butter, a small knob at a time, until the sauce is shiny. Heat for 15 sec at a time on 50% setting until the sauce resembles lightly whipped cream, stirring gently each time. Add a little pepper and lemon juice to taste. Serve warm with salmon, asparagus, vegetable entrées and fish dishes.

3 × 15ml tbsp (3tbsp) water
1 × 15ml tbsp (1tbsp) white wine vinegar or white wine
3 egg yolks
175g (6oz) butter, softened
salt and white pepper
few drops lemon juice

Cook's note: *Should the sauce begin to overcook and separate, remove from the microwave and stand in a bowl of cold water to prevent further cooking*

DO NOT FREEZE

Variations

Sauce mousseline
Mix 100ml (4fl oz) stiffly whipped double cream into the hollandaise sauce. Serve with sole, salmon and asparagus.

Mustard hollandaise
Mix some dijon mustard to taste into the hollandaise sauce. Serve with smoked salmon, mackerel or trout or spiced herrings.

Sauce vénitienne *(makes about 275ml/½pt)*
POWER LEVEL: 100% (FULL)

1 Place the onion, vinegar, herbs, wine and water into a bowl. Cook, uncovered, for about 5 min until the liquid quantity is reduced by about a quarter.
2 Leave to cool before whisking into the hollandaise sauce. Serve with mackerel, salmon or salmon trout.

3 × 15ml tbsp (3tbsp) finely chopped onion
1½ × 15ml tbsp (1½tbsp) white wine vinegar
1 × 15ml (1tbsp) finely chopped tarragon and chervil
100ml (4fl oz) white wine
100ml (4fl oz) water
1 quantity hollandaise sauce (above)

150ml (¼pt) olive oil
3 × 15ml tbsp (3tbsp) white wine vinegar
½ × 5ml tsp (½tsp) dry mustard
salt and freshly ground black pepper

French dressing *(makes about 175ml/6fl oz)*

Blend the oil, vinegar, mustard and seasoning by whisking together in a bowl or placing in a screw-top jar and shaking vigorously. Alternatively, blend in a liquidiser or food processor.

Vinaigrette dressing
Make a french dressing and beat in 1 × 15ml tbsp (1tbsp) finely chopped mixed herbs.

DO NOT FREEZE

225g (8oz) gooseberries
2 × 15ml tbsp (2tbsp) water
sugar to taste
salt and pepper
15g (½oz) butter
1 × 15ml tbsp (1tbsp) finely chopped mint leaves

Gooseberry and mint sauce *(makes about 200ml/7fl oz)*
POWER LEVEL: 100% (FULL)

1 Place the gooseberries in a bowl or dish with the water, sugar to taste and a little seasoning. Add the butter, cover and cook for 5–6 min until tender, stirring once or twice throughout.
2 Purée the sauce in a blender or food processor or rub through a sieve. Just before serving, stir in the chopped mint leaves. Serve with lamb.

675g (1½lb) cooking apples, sliced
25–40g (1–1½oz) butter
275ml (½pt) madeira
2 oranges, grated rind and strained juice
1 lemon, strained juice

Apple sauce with madeira *(makes about 275ml/½pt)*
POWER LEVEL: 100% (FULL)

1 Cook the apples with the butter in a covered dish or bowl for 10–12 min until tender, stirring 2–3 times throughout. Drain well and purée in a blender or food processor.
2 Heat the madeira and orange rind for 10–12 min, uncovered, until reduced by half, then stir in the apple purée. Cook, uncovered, until reduced and a thick consistency is reached.
3 Leave to cool before stirring in the lemon and orange juices. Serve with goose, duck or pork.

175g (6oz) bitter chocolate
1 × 5ml tsp (1tsp) butter
3–4 × 15ml tbsp (3–4tbsp) golden syrup
rum or brandy to taste
150ml (¼pt) thick cream

Chocolate cream sauce *(makes about 425ml/¾pt)*
POWER LEVEL: 100% (FULL)

1 Break up the chocolate and place in a bowl with the butter and syrup. Heat until melted, 2–3 min, stirring once halfway through.
2 Stir in a little rum or brandy to taste and the cream. Heat, uncovered, for 1–1½ min until just hot, without boiling. Serve hot or cold.

4 ripe peaches, halved and stoned
2 × 15ml tbsp (2tbsp) rum
2 × 5ml tsp (2tsp) maraschino
icing or caster sugar to taste

Peach sauce *(makes about 175ml/6fl oz)*
POWER LEVEL: 100% (FULL)

1 Place the peach halves into a shallow dish, cover and cook for 3–4 min until just softened. Remove the skins and purée in a blender or food processor, or purée first and then pass through a sieve to remove the skins.
2 Place the purée back into the dish and add the rum, maraschino and sugar to taste. Heat without boiling on 70% setting for 2–3 min, stirring once or twice throughout. Serve with vanilla or praline ice cream.

Raspberry sauce

Purée 225g (8oz) fresh ripe raspberries in a blender or food processor. Add 50–75g caster or icing sugar to taste, and flavour with the juice of a lemon and about 1 × 15ml tbsp (1tbsp) raspberry liqueur. Strain the purée through a sieve to remove the pips. Serve with puddings, ice creams or baked fruits.

Chaud-froid of Chicken (page 48)

150ml (¼pt) water
225g (8oz) granulated sugar
150ml (¼pt) hot water
1 lemon, finely pared rind
cinnamon stick
1 × 5ml tsp (1tsp) arrowroot
100g (4oz) preserved ginger,
    chopped

Ginger sauce (makes 425ml/³/4pt)
POWER LEVEL: 100% (FULL)

1 Place the water and sugar in a large heatproof jug or bowl. Heat, uncovered, for 2 min, stir, and heat for a further 2–3 min until the sugar is completely dissolved.
2 Heat for about 10 min until it is golden brown in colour. Watch the caramel carefully to ensure it doesn't burn.
3 Using an oven glove to protect your hand, gradually add the hot water to the caramel. Stir well and heat for 30 sec. Add the lemon rind and cinnamon stick and leave to infuse for 30 min.
4 Remove the lemon rind and cinnamon stick. Blend the arrowroot with a little ginger syrup or caramel and add to the caramel, stirring well.
5 Heat for 3–4 min, stirring every minute until thickened. Add the chopped ginger and serve with sponge puddings, ice cream or plain fruit desserts.

DO NOT FREEZE

1 vanilla pod
425ml (¾pt) milk
50g (2oz) caster sugar
2 eggs
2 egg yolks

Vanilla cream (makes about 550ml/1pt)
POWER LEVEL: 100% (FULL) AND 50%

1 Place the vanilla pod into a large jug with the milk. Bring to the boil on 100% (full) setting, about 6 min, then leave to cool slightly. Remove the vanilla pod.
2 Beat the sugar, eggs and egg yolks together and stir in the milk. Heat on 50% setting for 4–6 min, stirring every minute, until the cream has thickened sufficiently to coat the back of a spoon.
3 Strain the sauce through a fine mesh into a bowl and leave to cool.

DO NOT FREEZE

1 egg yolk
1 egg
2 × 15ml tbsp (2tbsp) double
    cream
1 × 15ml tbsp (1tbsp) caster
    sugar
1 × 15ml tbsp (1tbsp) cherry
    liqueur

Sweet mousseline sauce (makes about 150ml/¹/4pt)
POWER LEVEL: 100% (FULL)

1 Place all the ingredients in a small basin and whisk well to combine.
2 Place in the microwave and heat, uncovered, for 1–1½ min, whisking every 15–20 sec until creamy and frothy. Take care not to overcook.
3 Serve immediately over light sponge puddings, Christmas pudding or fruit desserts.

DO NOT FREEZE

25g (1oz) blanched almonds,
    chopped
100g (4oz) butter
100g (4oz) soft brown sugar
2 × 15ml tbsp (2tbsp) water

Praline sauce (makes about 275ml/¹/2pt)
POWER LEVEL: 100% (FULL)

1 Place the almonds onto a heatproof plate and heat, uncovered, for 5–6 min until toasted, shaking or stirring once halfway through.
2 Cut the butter into cubes and place in a large bowl with the sugar and water. Heat, uncovered, for 1½ min until the butter is just melted, then stir or whisk to dissolve the sugar. Heat for a further 15 sec if necessary and beat until smooth.
3 Cook, uncovered, for 1–2 min or until boiling then cook for 1 min. Stir well, add the almonds and serve warm with ice cream or sponge pudding.

Rice, pasta and pulses

Ravioli *(serves 4)*
POWER LEVEL: 100% (FULL) AND 70%

1 Heat the oil in a casserole dish on 100% (full) setting for 2 min, add the onion and cook, covered, for 2–3 min. Add the minced pork, mix well and cook, covered, for 4 min, stirring once throughout.
2 Add the smoked pork or ham, salt, pepper, spices and the tomato purée and stir well. Cover and cook for 10–12 min on 70% setting.
3 Spread half the sheets of lasagne out on a board and brush with the beaten egg. Place teaspoonfuls of the filling on the lasagne, allowing sufficient room to make about 4 ravioli from each sheet. Place another sheet of lasagne over the meat and press down well, forming the ravioli parcels. Seal the edges and cut into squares using a pastry cutter.
4 Place the ravioli into a large dish. Heat the milk in a bowl or jug for 3 min on 100% (full) setting, season with salt and pepper and add the fresh herbs. Pour the milk over the pasta, cover the dish and cook for 6–8 min.
5 Remove the ravioli to a warmed serving plate using a draining spoon. Making sure there is ample room for expansion, heat the milk for 5–6 min on 100% (full) setting in the microwave – it should reduce and thicken slightly; stir once or twice while heating. Add the cream and whisk well.
6 Heat the sauce on 100% (full) for 1–2 min, if necessary, and spoon it over the ravioli. Sprinkle with parmesan cheese before serving.

DO NOT FREEZE

2 × 15ml tbsp (2tbsp) olive oil
1 small onion, chopped
225g (8oz) lean pork, minced
100g (4oz) smoked pork or ham, minced
salt and freshly ground black pepper
1–2 × 5ml tsp (1–2tsp) each mace and cloves
1 × 15ml tbsp (1tbsp) tomato purée
18 sheets, approximately 350g (12oz), fresh lasagne
1 egg, beaten
425ml (¾pt) milk
2 × 15ml tbsp (2tbsp) chopped fresh mixed herbs
150ml (¼pt) soured cream
for serving: grated parmesan cheese

Pasta al pesto *(serves 4)*
POWER LEVEL: 100% (FULL)

1 Roughly chop the basil leaves – fresh basil, if available, gives a much better colour to this dish than dried basil. Mix together the basil, garlic and a good pinch of salt to make a paste.
2 Add the parmesan cheese and the olive oil and mix well. Season the pesto to taste with the black pepper and the pine nuts.
3 Place the tagliatelle in a large bowl with the oil and salt and cover with boiling water. Cover and cook for 5 min, allow to stand for 3 min and then drain.
4 Toss the tagliatelle in the pesto and serve immediately as a starter.

2 cups fresh basil leaves or 1 × 15ml tbsp (1tbsp) dried basil
3 cloves garlic, crushed
salt and freshly ground black pepper
75g (3oz) parmesan cheese, grated
150ml (¼pt) olive oil
50g (2oz) pine kernels
225g (8oz) tagliatelle
1 × 15ml tbsp (1tbsp) oil
1 × 5ml tsp (1tsp) salt
boiling water

Pistachio and raisin pilaff *(serves 4–6)*
POWER LEVEL: 100% (FULL)

1 Melt the butter in a casserole dish for 1–2 min and add the onion and garlic. Cover and cook for 4 min, stirring once throughout.
2 Stir in the rice and the raisins and add the boiling stock. Cover and cook for 12–15 min, and allow to stand for 5 min.
3 Stir in the nuts and season to taste with salt and freshly ground black pepper.
4 Serve sprinkled with chopped coriander leaves.

50g (2oz) butter
1 large onion, sliced (use a red onion if possible)
1 clove garlic, crushed
225g (8oz) basmati rice, washed
75g (3oz) seedless raisins
550ml (1pt) white chicken stock (page 20)
100g (4oz) pistachio nuts, shelled
salt and freshly ground black pepper
for garnish: chopped coriander leaves

2 × 15ml tbsp (2tbsp) olive oil
1 onion, chopped
1 small red pepper, deseeded
    and cut into strips
450g (1lb) chicken breast fillet,
    diced
100g (4oz) lean pork, diced
175g (6oz) squid, cleaned and
    sliced
2 large tomatoes, skinned,
    deseeded and chopped
175g (6oz) chorizo sausage,
    sliced
225g (8oz) live mussels, cleaned
    and scrubbed
50g (2oz) french beans, cut into
    5cm (2in) lengths
100g (4oz) shelled peas
1 clove garlic, crushed
powdered saffron
350g (12oz) long-grain rice
325ml (12fl oz) boiling water
salt and freshly ground black
    pepper
100g (4oz) peeled prawns
for garnish: a few large or
    mediterranean unpeeled
    prawns

Paella valenciana (*serves 6*)   *colour opposite*
POWER LEVEL: 100% (FULL)

1 Heat the oil in a very large bowl for 2 min. Add the onion and pepper, stir well, cover and cook for 3 min. Add the chicken and pork and cook for a further 6–8 min, stirring once throughout.
2 Add the squid and tomatoes, mix well, cover and cook for 6–8 min. Add the chorizo and mussels and cook, uncovered, for 5–8 min until all the mussels have opened. Stir once during cooking.
3 Add the beans and peas, crushed garlic and saffron to colour, and stir in the rice. Add the boiling water, stir well, cover the dish and cook for 15 min.
4 Season well and stir in the prawns. Cover and cook for a further 5 min and allow to stand for 5 min. Garnish with a few large unpeeled prawns before serving.

DO NOT FREEZE

Cook's note: *This is very much a Spanish country dish with many local variations, cooked and served straight from a two-handled iron pan from which the dish takes its name – paella. For the microwave, use a suitable container to cook and serve the paella or transfer onto a serving dish. For special occasions, go to town on the garnishing by cooking a few extra mussels and arranging them around the edge of the dish with the prawns. Finally, garnish with plenty of lemon wedges*

225g (8oz) italian or short-grain
    rice
boiling water
40–50g (1½–2oz) parmesan
    cheese, grated
2 small eggs, lightly beaten
275ml (½pt) thick tomato
    sauce (page 74)
salt and freshly ground black
    pepper
50g (2oz) bel paese cheese,
    finely diced
50g (2oz) cooked ham,
    prosciutto or chicken, finely
    diced
flour
50g (2oz) fresh breadcrumbs
oil for deep frying
3–4 × 15ml tbsp (3–4tbsp)
    single cream
for garnish: fresh sage, basil or
    mint leaves

Arancini (*serves 4*)
POWER LEVEL: 100% (FULL)

These crisp rice balls or 'oranges', to give their literal translation, are prepared in the microwave and then conventionally deep fried in hot oil. Serve them as a lunch or supper dish

1 Place the rice in a large bowl and add sufficient boiling water to cover. Cover the dish with a lid or pierced clingfilm and cook for about 15 min. Leave to stand for 3 min and then drain and rinse the rice thoroughly.
2 Return the rice to the bowl and stir in the parmesan cheese, the eggs, 1 × 15ml tbsp (1tbsp) tomato sauce and salt to taste. Mix well together and leave until cold.
3 In another bowl, place 2 × 15ml tbsp (2tbsp) tomato sauce, the diced cheese and ham and seasoning to taste. Mix well together.
4 Take a level 15ml tbsp (tbsp) of the rice mixture and mould it in the palm of the hand using a little flour to help prevent sticking. Place 2 × 5ml tsp (2tsp) of the cheese mixture into the hollow and top with a little more rice mixture. Form into balls about 4cm (1½in) in diameter. Repeat to make about 12 balls.
5 Coat the balls thickly in the fresh breadcrumbs and fry them in hot oil, about 2 or 3 at a time, until golden brown.
6 Drain the arancini on absorbent paper and keep hot. Just before serving, garnish each ball with herb leaves. Add the single cream to the remaining tomato sauce, reheat for 2 min and serve separately.

Paella Valenciana (above)

Spiced chick peas and sweet potato *(serves 4)*
POWER LEVEL: 100% (FULL) AND 50%

225g (8oz) chick peas
boiling water
50g (2oz) ghee or clarified butter
1 large onion, finely sliced
2 cloves garlic, crushed
1 × 5ml tsp (1tsp) each turmeric
   and ground ginger
½ × 5ml tsp (½tsp) chilli
   powder
1 × 15ml tbsp (1tbsp) coriander
   seeds, crushed
1 sweet potato, about 350g
   (12oz), peeled and diced
salt and freshly ground black
   pepper
150ml (¼pt) natural yoghurt
   or soured cream
for garnish: coriander leaves

1 Place the chick peas in a large bowl and cover them with boiling water. Cover the bowl and heat for 5 min on 100% (full) setting and allow to stand for 1 hr. Drain.
2 Return the chick peas to the bowl, cover with fresh boiling water and cover the dish. Cook for 10 min on 100% (full) and a further 25 min on 50% setting or until tender. Drain.
3 Heat the ghee or clarified butter in a casserole dish for 2 min on 100% (full). Add the onion and garlic, mix well, cover and cook for 3 min, stirring once during cooking. Stir in the spices and sweet potato, cover and cook for 5–6 min, stirring once halfway through. Season well with salt and black pepper.
4 Add the chick peas, stir well, cover and heat for 4–5 min, stirring once, until piping hot.
5 Stir in the yoghurt or soured cream and heat, uncovered, for 1–2 min. Serve garnished with coriander leaves.

Flageolet and prawn crêpes *(serves 4)*
POWER LEVEL: 100% (FULL), 70% AND 50%
CONVENTIONAL HOTPLATE

175g (6oz) flageolet beans
boiling water
1 egg
425ml (¾pt) milk
100g (4oz) plain flour
salt and freshly ground black
   pepper
oil for frying
25g (1oz) butter
25g (1oz) flour
150ml (¼pt) white wine
1 × 15ml tbsp (1tbsp) chopped
   fresh tarragon
350g (12oz) peeled prawns
75g (3oz) gruyère cheese,
   grated
150ml (¼pt) soured cream
for garnish: slices of lime and a
   few unpeeled prawns

1 Place the flageolets in a bowl and add sufficient boiling water to cover. Cover the bowl and cook for 5 min on 100% (full) setting and allow to stand for 1 hr before draining.
2 While the flageolets are soaking, prepare the pancakes. Blend the egg and 275ml (½pt) milk in a liquidiser or food processor, add the plain flour and ¼ × 5ml tsp (¼tsp) salt and blend thoroughly.
3 Heat a little oil in a frypan and cook the pancakes, separating them between pieces of kitchen paper until required and adding more oil to the pan as necessary.
4 Cover the flageolets with fresh boiling water, cover the dish and cook for 10 min on 100% (full) setting and a further 25–35 min on 50% until the beans are tender.
5 Melt the butter in a large jug or bowl for 1–2 min, add the flour and mix well. Gradually add the remaining milk and the wine. Heat for 4–5 min, stirring every minute until the sauce is thickened and boiling. Add the tarragon, prawns, drained flageolets and the cheese. Adjust the seasoning to taste with salt and freshly ground black pepper.
6 Fill the pancakes with the prawn mixture, roll or fold each one and place onto a serving plate or dish. Cover with pierced clingfilm and cook for 6–7 min on 70% setting until piping hot.
7 Pour the cream over the pancakes and heat for 2–3 min on 70% setting until heated through. Serve garnished with slices of lime and a few unpeeled prawns.

Cassoulet from toulouse (serves 4–6)
POWER LEVEL: 100% (FULL), 70% AND 50%

Like the paella from Spain, the cassoulet varies from region to region in France. It is a very substantial dish to be served on cold winter days

1 Place the beans in a large dish and add sufficient boiling water to cover. Cover and cook for 5 min on 100% (full) setting and allow to stand for 1 hr before draining.
2 Place the duck or goose joint in a covered casserole dish and cook 10–12 min on 70% setting. Allow to cool slightly then skin and bone the joint. Leave the fat and juices in the bottom of the casserole dish.
3 Add the garlic and carrots to the dish, stir well in the fat and cook for 4 min on 100% (full) setting, stirring once throughout. Dice the duck or goose and add it to the dish with the tomatoes, sausage, beans and salt and pepper to taste.
4 Pour the boiling stock into the dish to cover the beans, add the bouquet garni, cover and cook for 10 min on 100% (full) and a further 35–45 min on 50% setting, until the beans are tender stirring occasionally. Adjust the seasoning, remove the bouquet garni and serve with french bread.

225g (8oz) haricot beans
boiling water
450g (1lb) joint duck or goose
3 cloves garlic, crushed
2 carrots, sliced
2 tomatoes, skinned, deseeded and chopped
225g (8oz) french garlic sausage, diced
salt and freshly ground black pepper
425ml (¾pt) boiling chicken stock (page 20) approximately
1 bouquet garni
for serving: crusty french bread

Spaghetti alla carbonara (serves 4)
POWER LEVEL: 100% (FULL)

1 Place the spaghetti in a large oblong dish with a pinch of salt and the oil. Cover with boiling water, cover the dish and cook for 10 min. Leave to stand. The pasta will still be fairly firm. (If using an alternative or slightly smaller dish, the uncooked spaghetti should be pushed beneath the boiling water with a metal spoon until softened before cooking.)
2 Place the bacon on a plate, cover with kitchen paper towel and cook for 4–5 min until crispy.
3 Add the cream and half the parmesan to the beaten eggs with plenty of black pepper to taste.
4 Drain the spaghetti and place in a large bowl. Add the bacon and the egg mixture and stir well. Cook, uncovered, for 2–3 min, stirring every minute.
5 Serve immediately, sprinkled with the remaining parmesan cheese.

DO NOT FREEZE

350g (12oz) spaghetti
salt
1 × 15ml tbsp (1tbsp) oil
boiling water
100g (4oz) streaky bacon, derinded and diced
4 × 15ml tbsp (4tbsp) single cream
50g (2oz) parmesan cheese, grated
2 eggs, beaten
freshly ground black pepper

Tagliatelle with wild mushrooms (serves 3–4)
POWER LEVEL: 100% (FULL) AND 70%

1 Place the tagliatelle in a large bowl with a pinch of salt and 1 × 15ml tbsp (1tbsp) oil. Add sufficient boiling water to cover. Cover the bowl and cook for 5 min on 100% (full) setting, stand for 3 min and then drain.
2 Place the butter and olive oil in a medium-size casserole dish and heat for 2 min or until the butter has melted. Add the mushrooms and garlic and toss in the butter and oil. Cover and cook for 4–5 min, stirring once half-way through.
3 Season the mushrooms to taste with salt and freshly ground black pepper, and add the cream.
4 Toss the tagliatelle in a little oil or melted butter and freshly ground black pepper to taste. Spoon the mushrooms and cream over the pasta and gently shake the dish to coat the noodles with the sauce.
5 Reheat if necessary for 3 min on 70% setting, covered, and garnish with freshly chopped parsley before serving.

225g (8oz) tagliatelli verdi
salt and freshly ground black pepper
1 × 15ml tbsp (1tbsp) oil
boiling water
50g (2oz) butter
1 × 15ml tbsp (1tbsp) olive oil
225–275g (8–10oz) wild mushrooms, sliced
1 clove garlic, crushed
150–275ml (¼–½pt) soured or double cream
oil or melted butter
for garnish: freshly chopped parsley

2 × 50g (2oz) cans anchovy
   fillets, drained
milk
450g (1lb) prepared cauliflower,
   cut into tiny florets
2 × 15ml tbsp (2tbsp) salted
   water
350g (12oz) pasta shapes
   eg farfalle 'butterflies'
salt and freshly ground black
   pepper
1 × 15ml tbsp (1tbsp) oil
boiling water
2 × 15ml tbsp (2tbsp) olive oil
1 large onion, chopped
1 clove garlic, crushed
225g (8oz) tomatoes, skinned
   and chopped
2 × 15ml tbsp (2tbsp) cream
for garnish: parsley sprigs
for serving: green salad

Pasta with cauliflower and anchovy sauce *(serves 4–6)*
POWER LEVEL: 100% (FULL)   *colour opposite*

1   Soak the anchovy fillets in milk while preparing the other ingredients. Place the prepared cauliflower in a dish with the salted water, cover and cook for 6–8 min, stirring once throughout.
2   Place the pasta in a large bowl with a pinch of salt and the 1 × 15ml tbsp (1tbsp) oil. Add sufficient boiling water to cover the pasta. Cover the bowl and cook for 8–10 min until tender but still with a 'bite'. Allow to stand for a few minutes and then drain.
3   Heat the olive oil in a dish for 2 min, add the onion and garlic and cook, covered, for 3–4 min, stirring once halfway through.
4   Add the cauliflower, tomatoes, drained anchovy fillets and plenty of black pepper. Cook, uncovered, for 10–15 min until the sauce is reduced and thickened, stirring occasionally.
5   Add the pasta to the sauce and toss well. Reheat for 2–3 min if necessary, stir in the cream and add more seasoning to taste. Garnish with parsley and serve immediately with a green salad.

450g (1lb) leaf spinach, stalks
   removed
freshly ground black pepper
2 × 15ml tbsp (2tbsp) olive oil
1 onion, finely chopped
1 clove garlic, crushed
350g (12oz) lean veal, minced
2 × 15ml tbsp (2tbsp) chopped
   fresh basil
2 × 15ml tbsp (2tbsp) tomato
   purée
425ml (¾pt) white wine,
   approximately
salt
18–20 easy-cook cannelloni
   tubes
1 × 400g (14oz) can chopped
   tomatoes
100g (4oz) cheddar cheese,
   grated
25g (1oz) parmesan cheese,
   grated

Veal stuffed cannelloni *(serves 4–6)*   *colour opposite*
POWER LEVEL: 100% (FULL) AND 70%

1   Wash the spinach well in several changes of water and shake dry. Place it in a large bowl, cover and cook on 100% (full) setting for 6–8 min, stirring once during cooking. Drain the spinach in a colander, pressing well and chopping it to remove excess water. Season well with black pepper.
2   Heat the oil in a large bowl for 2 min, add the onion and garlic, cover and cook for 3 min. Add the veal, mix well together and cook for a further 4 min, stirring once.
3   Add the spinach, half the basil, tomato purée and 150ml (¼pt) wine to the bowl with a little salt and pepper to taste. Cover and cook for 20 min on 70% setting, stirring once halfway through. Adjust the seasoning to taste.
4   Fill the cannelloni tubes with the veal stuffing and arrange them in a single layer in the bottom of a large shallow dish.
5   Mix together the tomatoes, some salt and pepper, the rest of the basil and the remaining 275ml (½pt) wine. Pour over the cannelloni, adding extra wine, if necessary, to cover the pasta. Cover the dish and cook for 20–25 min on 100% (full) setting.
6   Mix together the cheddar and parmesan cheeses and add some black pepper. Sprinkle over the cannelloni and heat, uncovered, for 3–4 min or until the cheese has melted. Alternatively, brown the top of the dish under a hot grill.

*Pasta with Cauliflower and Anchovy
Sauce (above); Veal Stuffed
Canelloni (above)*

1 small piece root ginger, grated
2 cloves garlic, crushed
1 small onion, grated
1 × 5ml tsp (1tsp) salt
150ml (¼pt) natural yoghurt
2 × 15ml tbsp (2tbsp) ghee or
  clarified butter
4 cloves
8 peppercorns
1 cinnamon stick
1 brown cardamom
1 large onion, finely sliced
2 tomatoes, skinned and
  chopped
225g (8oz) basmati or long-
  grain rice
100g (4oz) cashew nuts
100g (4oz) blanched almonds
425ml (¾pt) boiling chicken
  stock (page 20)
for garnish: chopped coriander
  leaves, optional
for serving: mixed vegetable
  curry sauce (below)

2 × 15ml tbsp (2tbsp) ghee or
  clarified butter
1 large onion, finely sliced
2 cloves garlic, crushed
1 large aubergine, trimmed,
  halved and sliced
2 large courgettes, trimmed
  and finely sliced
1 green chilli, deseeded and
  finely chopped
75g (3oz) shelled peas
1 bay leaf
6 cloves
6 peppercorns
1 cinnamon stick
1 × 5ml tsp (1tsp) turmeric
2 × 5ml tsp (2tsp) ground
  cumin
¼–½ × 5ml tsp (¼–½tsp)
  chilli powder
salt to taste
2 tomatoes, skinned and sliced
50g (2oz) mushrooms, sliced
for garnish: chopped coriander
  or parsley, optional

Almonds and cashew biriani (*serves 4*)   *colour page 47*
POWER LEVEL: 100% (FULL)

1 Pound together in a pestle and mortar the ginger, garlic and grated onion with the salt. Add the yoghurt and stir well.
2 Heat the ghee or clarified butter in a casserole dish for 2 min, add the spices, stir well and cook for 2 min. Stir in the yoghurt paste and cook, covered, for 2 min.
3 Add the sliced onion and the tomatoes, cover and cook for 3 min.
4 Stir the rice into the dish with half the cashews and almonds. Add the boiling stock, stir, cover and cook for 15–18 min. Allow to stand for 5 min.
5 Place the remaining almonds and cashews on a microwave heatproof plate and cook for 4–5 min until browned, tossing them over once halfway through. Scatter the nuts over the biriani and garnish with chopped coriander leaves if required, before serving with a vegetable curry sauce.

Cook's note: *Serve this Indian dish with a salad of chopped onions, tomatoes and green chillies, adding a little sugar, salt and vinegar to taste*

Vegetable curry (*serves 4*)   *colour page 47*
POWER LEVEL: 100% (FULL)

1 Place the ghee or clarified butter into a large bowl or casserole dish and heat in the microwave for 1 min. Stir in the onion, cover and cook for 3 min.
2 Add the garlic, aubergine, courgettes, chilli, peas, bay leaf and the spices. Mix well together, cover and cook for 10–12 min, stirring once or twice throughout, until the vegetables are tender.
3 Add salt to taste and stir in the tomatoes and mushrooms. Continue to cook for a further 4–5 min, uncovered, until hot through.
4 Remove the bay leaf and serve straight away, garnished with coriander or parsley if required.

Desserts

Chocolate roulade (serves 6)
POWER LEVEL: 100% (FULL)

1 Whisk the egg yolks with the 75g (3oz) caster sugar until very thick. Sift the flour, cocoa and baking powder into the egg yolks, then fold in. Mix in the water. Whisk the egg whites until stiff, then carefully fold them, a little at a time, into the cocoa mixture.
2 Pour the sponge mixture into a thin 22cm (8½in) square plastic microwave dish. Cook for 3 min on 100% (full) setting, until well risen and firm to the touch, yet still slightly moist on the top. Turn the dish during cooking if necessary and do not overcook. Allow the sponge to stand for 1 min, then turn it onto a sheet of sugared greaseproof paper and allow to cool.
3 Whisk the cream with the kirsch and the remaining sugar until it will hold soft peaks.
4 Spread half of the cream over the chocolate sponge, then carefully roll the sponge up, using the paper as a guide.
5 Place the chocolate roll on a flat serving dish, then spread the remaining cream all over it. Mark the cream into swirls, then decorate with chocolate curls. If liked, the roll may be decorated with stoned black cherries.

3 eggs, size 2, separated
75g (3oz) plus 1 × 15ml tbsp (1tbsp) caster sugar
25g (1oz) plain flour
15g (½oz) cocoa
¼ × 5ml tsp (¼tsp) baking powder
2 × 5ml tsp (2tsp) cold water
275ml (½pt) double cream
2 × 15ml tbsp (2tbsp) kirsch
for decoration: chocolate curls, or grated chocolate, and stoned black cherries, optional

Creamy rice with apricot sauce (serves 4) *colour on back cover*
POWER LEVEL: 50% AND 100% (FULL)

1 Put the rice into a sieve and rinse well under a cold tap. Drain well.
2 Put the rice, milk, sugar and vanilla into a large heat-resistant dish. Cover the dish with clingfilm, pulling back 1 corner to vent. Cook on 50% setting for 45–50 min, until the rice is cooked and almost all of the milk has been absorbed, stirring frequently.
3 When the rice is cooked, cover the surface closely with greaseproof paper or clingfilm to prevent a skin forming. Allow to cool, then refrigerate until quite cold.
4 Whisk the cream until it will hold soft peaks. Fold the cream into the cold rice, then spoon it into 4 attractive serving dishes, or glasses. Refrigerate while making the sauce.
5 To make the sauce: cut the drained apricots into slices. Put the butter, sugar, and orange juice into a heat-resistant mixing bowl. Cook on 100% (full) setting for 1 min. Add the apricots and cook for a further 2 min. Stir in the grand marnier, then pour into a serving jug or bowl.
6 Serve the rice with the hot apricot sauce.

40g (1½oz) pudding rice
550ml (1pt) milk
25g (1oz) caster sugar
1 × 5ml tsp (1tsp) vanilla essence
150ml (¼pt) double cream

for the apricot sauce:
425g (15oz) can apricots in natural juice, drained
15g (½oz) butter
25g (1oz) caster sugar
2 × 15ml tbsp (2tbsp) fresh orange juice
2 × 15ml tbsp (2tbsp) grand marnier

Chocolate creams (serves 6)
POWER LEVEL: 100% (FULL)

1 Put the chocolate, milk and coffee into a heat-resistant mixing bowl. Heat for 2½ min, then stir until the chocolate melts.
2 Put the cream and vanilla into a heat-resistant mixing bowl. Heat for 1 min.
3 Very lightly whisk the egg yolks and the whole egg together, but do not make the mixture frothy. Stir in the chocolate-flavoured milk and the vanilla cream. Strain the custard mixture into six 150ml (¼pt) ramekin or soufflé dishes.

100g (4oz) plain chocolate, broken into small pieces
275ml (½pt) milk
2 × 5ml tsp (2tsp) instant coffee
275ml (½pt) single cream
few drops vanilla essence
5 egg yolks, size 2
1 whole egg
for decoration: whipped cream and grated chocolate, optional

4 Place the dishes, evenly spaced apart, in a circle in the microwave oven. Cook for 4½–5 min, giving the dishes a quarter turn every minute, until the chocolate mixture is just set. Allow to cool, then refrigerate for at least 3 hr before serving or use the next day.

Cook's note: *These little chocolate creams are very rich and may be served plain. But, if you prefer, they can be decorated with a swirl of cream and grated chocolate*

DO NOT FREEZE

for the filling:
225g (8oz) plain chocolate, broken into small pieces
550ml (1pt) milk
50g (2oz) cornflour
2 eggs, size 2, separated
25g (1oz) caster sugar

for the choux pastry:
75g (3oz) butter, cut into pieces
215ml (7½fl oz) water
100g (4oz) plain flour
a pinch of salt
3 eggs, size 2, beaten
icing sugar for sifting

for the vanilla cream:
275ml (½pt) double cream
1 × 5ml tsp (1tsp) vanilla essence
1 × 15ml tbsp (1tbsp) caster sugar

Chocolate filled profiteroles (*serves 6–8*)   *colour opposite*
POWER LEVEL: 50% AND 100% (FULL)
CONVENTIONAL OVEN TEMPERATURE: 180°C (350°F) MARK 4

1 To make the filling: put the chocolate and three-quarters of the milk into a large heat-resistant mixing bowl. Heat on 50% setting for 3–4 min until the milk is very hot and the chocolate has melted, stirring well every minute.
2 In another large mixing bowl, blend the cornflour with the egg yolks and the remaining milk. Stir in the caster sugar and the hot, chocolate-flavoured milk. Cook on 100% (full) setting for about 8 min until the custard thickens and no trace of raw cornflour remains, stirring well every 2 min with a wire whisk. The mixture will be very thick.
3 Whisk the egg whites until very stiff. Fold, a little at a time, into the hot chocolate mixture. Cover the surface closely with greaseproof paper or clingfilm to prevent a skin forming. Cool, then refrigerate until quite cold.
4 To make the choux buns: line two baking sheets with non-stick baking paper.
5 Put the butter and water into a large bowl and heat on 50% setting until the butter melts. Bring to the boil on 100% (full) setting, then quickly add the flour and salt. Beat the mixture well until it forms a ball, heating for a further 15–30 sec if necessary. Allow to cool slightly, then gradually beat in the eggs, beating well after each addition. The choux paste should be very shiny.
6 Put the choux paste into a large piping bag fitted with a large star nozzle. Pipe about 40 small rosettes on the lined baking sheets, spacing them well apart.
7 Bake the choux buns in the preheated oven for 25–30 min until they are well risen and golden brown. Remove the buns from the oven and pierce each one through the base with a small knife to allow the steam to escape. Return to the oven for 5 min to dry completely. Remove from the baking sheets to cooling racks to cool.
8 Whisk the cold chocolate mixture until smooth, then spoon it into a large piping bag fitted with a small plain nozzle. Fill each choux bun with chocolate mixture, piping it into the bun through the small hole made in the base.
9 Pile the profiteroles up in a serving bowl and sift with icing sugar. Very lightly whisk the cream with the vanilla and caster sugar, then pour it into a serving jug, or bowl. Serve the profiteroles with the vanilla cream poured over them.

DO NOT FREEZE

Cook's note: *An alternative serving idea is to place a thin layer of vanilla cream onto individual serving plates and pipe fine lines of reserved chocolate cream over the top. Use a skewer or sharp knife and pull it across the chocolate lines in opposite directions to form a feathered effect. Arrange the profiteroles on top, allowing 2–4 per person (see colour opposite)*

Chocolate Filled Profiteroles (above)

175g (6oz) granulated sugar

150ml (¼pt) and 3 × 15ml tbsp (3tbsp) water

450g (1lb) fresh pineapple flesh

8 egg yolks, size 2

1 envelope of gelatin

275ml (½pt) double cream

2 egg whites, size 2

for the sauce:

450g (1lb) fresh loganberries or raspberries, (or frozen fruit, thawed)

100g (4oz) caster sugar

2 × 15ml tbsp (2tbsp) kirsch

for decoration: 150ml (¼pt) double cream, whipped and fresh loganberries, or raspberries

Pineapple mousse with loganberry sauce *(serves 8)*

POWER LEVEL: 70% AND 100% (FULL)

1 Put the granulated sugar into a small mixing bowl with 150ml (¼pt) water, heat for 2 min on 70% setting and stir until every granule of sugar is dissolved. Bring to the boil on 100% (full) and boil for 1 min. Remove from the microwave and allow to cool.

2 Very finely chop the pineapple flesh (do not purée in a blender).

3 Whisk the egg yolks until they are very light and thick, then gradually whisk in the cooled sugar syrup. Strain the mixture through a nylon sieve into a large heat-resistant mixing bowl.

4 Stir the pineapple into the egg-yolk mixture. Cook, uncovered, on 70% setting for 25 min, stirring every 3 min, until the custard is thickened slightly.

5 Put 3 × 15ml tbsp (3tbsp) cold water into a basin, sprinkle the gelatin over the top and leave to stand for about 1 min until the gelatin swells and looks opaque.

6 Add the gelatin to the hot pineapple mixture and stir until dissolved. Allow to cool.

7 Whisk the cream until it will just hold soft peaks. Whisk the egg whites until stiff.

8 Fold the whipped cream into the pineapple mixture, then carefully fold in the egg whites. Pour the mousse mixture into a 1·1 litre (2pt) ring mould, or decorative mould. Refrigerate for at least 3 hr until set.

9 To make the sauce: put the loganberries or raspberries into a mixing bowl and sprinkle with caster sugar. Cover and leave to stand for at least 1 hr.

10 Press the fruit through a nylon sieve or blend in a food processor to make a purée, then stir in the kirsch. Pour into a serving jug and chill.

11 To unmould the mousse: dip the mould up to the rim in very hot water for 5 sec only. Place a serving plate on top of the mould, then invert the mould and the plate together. Carefully lift off the mould.

12 Decorate the mousse with piped whipped cream and fresh loganberries or raspberries. Serve with the chilled sauce.

Hot strawberries *(serves 2–3)*   *colour on back cover*
POWER LEVEL: 100% (FULL)

1   Put the water into a shallow, glass heat-resistant dish or large bowl, add the sugar and stir until it dissolves. Cook for about 5 min until the sugar turns a golden caramel colour.
2   Remove the dish from the oven and very carefully pour in the grand marnier. Arrange the strawberries in a single layer on top of the caramel. Cook for 2–2½ min, turning the strawberries and repositioning them after 1 min.
3   Allow the strawberries to stand for 2 min before serving in the dish or in individual glasses. Serve with lightly whipped cream, or ice cream.

Cook's note: *Watch the strawberries during cooking to ensure they do not overcook and collapse, particularly if very ripe*

DO NOT FREEZE

2 × 15ml tbsp (2tbsp) boiling water
100g (4oz) caster sugar
3 × 15ml tbsp (3tbsp) grand marnier
450g (1lb) even-sized strawberries, hulled and cut into halves if large
for serving: lightly whipped fresh double cream, or ice cream

Tipsy chestnut gâteau *(serves 8)*   *colour page 107*
POWER LEVEL: 100% (FULL)

1   To make the sponge: whisk the eggs and caster sugar together until they are very light and thick, and the mixture will hold a trail for at least 5 sec.
2   Sift the flour, salt and baking powder over the surface of the whisked mixture, then lightly fold it in. Gradually fold in the melted butter.
3   Divide the sponge mixture equally between two 20cm (8in) microwave sponge dishes. Cook each sponge for 3 min, until well risen and firm to the touch, but still slightly moist on the top. Allow to stand for 1 min before turning onto a cooling rack to cool.
4   Cut each sponge cake in half horizontally. Whisk the cream until it is thick, but not buttery.
5   Place one of the sponge layers on a flat serving plate. Spoon a quarter of the rum over the sponge, then spread with a third of the chestnut purée. Spread 2 × 15ml tbsp (2tbsp) of cream over the purée, then place a second layer of sponge on top. Repeat until the sponges are used up. End with a layer of sponge, then spoon on the remaining rum.
6   Completely cover the sponge layers with the remaining cream, in swirls. Refrigerate the gâteau for at least 3–4 hr before serving. Decorate with slices of marrons glacés, if liked.

for the sponge:
4 eggs, size 2
100g (4oz) caster sugar
100g (4oz) plain flour
a pinch of salt
½ × 5ml tsp (½tsp) baking powder
50g (2oz) unsalted butter, melted and cooled

for the filling and topping:
425ml (¾pt) double cream
150ml (¼pt) rum
450g (1lb) can crème de marrons (sweetened chestnut purée)
for decoration: marrons glacés, optional

Crème brulée *(serves 4–6)*
POWER LEVEL: 100% (FULL)
CONVENTIONAL GRILL

1   Lightly mix the egg yolks, vanilla essence and caster sugar together.
2   Pour the creams into a heat-resistant mixing bowl. Heat for 2 min until hot, but not boiling.
3   Pour the hot cream into the egg yolks, stirring well. Strain the mixture through a nylon sieve into a heat-resistant mixing bowl. Cook for 2½–3 min until the custard just begins to thicken, stirring every 45 sec with a wire whisk.
4   Pour the custard immediately into a heat-resistant serving dish. Allow to cool, then refrigerate overnight until quite set.
5   Sprinkle caster sugar over the top of the custard to make a thin layer. Allow the sugar to settle on top of the custard for about 10 min then cook under a very hot grill for 2–3 min until the sugar melts and turns golden brown. Serve immediately.

DO NOT FREEZE

6 egg yolks, size 2
½ × 5ml tsp (½tsp) vanilla essence
1 × 15ml tbsp (1tbsp) caster sugar and extra for sprinkling
275ml (½pt) double cream
275ml (½pt) single cream

275ml (½pt) water
225g (8oz) granulated sugar
thinly pared rind and strained
  juice of 1 large lemon
8 medium-sized pears
2 × 15ml tbsp (2tbsp) kirsch,
  optional

for the sauce:
450g (1lb) fresh strawberries,
  hulled, or frozen strawberries,
  thawed
100g (4oz) caster sugar
for decoration: angelica leaves
for serving: whipped cream,
  optional

Poached pears with strawberry sauce *(serves 4)*   *colour opposite*
POWER LEVEL: 100% (FULL)

1   Put the water, sugar, lemon rind and juice into a very large heat-resistant mixing bowl. Cook for 8 min, stirring well after 4 min.
2   Carefully peel the pears, using a potato peeler, leaving the stalks on. Place the pears in the hot sugar syrup. Cook for 12–15 min, turning the pears every 3 min, until the pears are only just cooked when pierced with the tip of a knife.
3   Cool the pears in the syrup, then stir in the kirsch, if required, and refrigerate until well chilled.
4   To make the sauce: put the strawberries into a mixing bowl and sprinkle with the sugar. Cover and leave to stand for at least 1 hr.
5   Press the strawberries through a nylon sieve to make a purée or blend in a food processor. Coat the pears with the sauce and decorate with angelica leaves or hand the sauce separately. Serve with whipped cream if liked.

100g (4oz) plain chocolate
7 × 15ml tbsp (7tbsp) cold
  water
25g (1oz) unsalted butter
4 eggs, size 1, separated
50g (2oz) caster sugar
1 envelope of gelatin
150ml (¼pt) double cream

for the topping:
25g (1oz) plain chocolate
1 × 15ml tbsp (1tbsp) cold
  water
150ml (¼pt) double cream
for decoration: chocolate curls,
  grated chocolate and small
  chocolate leaves, optional

Chocolate soufflé *(serves 6)*   *colour opposite*
POWER LEVEL: 50% AND 100% (FULL)

1   To make the soufflé: prepare a 15cm (6in) soufflé dish by cutting a double strip of greaseproof paper long enough to go around the dish and one and a half times the depth of the dish in width. Secure the paper around the dish with sellotape or string. Stand the dish on a flat plate.
2   Break the chocolate into small pieces and put them into a small heat-resistant mixing bowl with 4 × 15ml tbsp (4tbsp) cold water. Heat on 50% setting for 1½ min, add the butter and stir halfway through. Stir until smooth. Allow to cool but not set.
3   Whisk the egg yolks and caster sugar together until they are very thick and creamy. Whisk in the cooled chocolate.
4   Put 3 × 15ml tbsp (3tbsp) cold water into a small mixing bowl, sprinkle the gelatin evenly over the surface and leave to stand for 1 min, until the gelatin swells and looks opaque.
5   Whisk the cream until it will only just hold soft peaks. Whisk the egg whites until stiff. Heat the gelatin on 100% (full) setting for 30–40 sec until it is melted and very hot.
6   Whisk the hot gelatin into the chocolate mixture. Fold in the cream, then quickly and carefully fold in the egg whites. Pour the soufflé mixture into the prepared dish. Refrigerate for 2–3 hr until set.
7   To make the topping: break the chocolate into small pieces and put them into a small mixing bowl with the cold water. Heat on 50% setting for about 1 min until the chocolate softens and looks shiny. Stir until smooth, then allow to cool but not set.
8   Whisk the cream until it will hold soft peaks. Place half the cream into a piping bag fitted with a star nozzle. Fold the cooled chocolate into the rest.
9   Carefully remove the paper from the soufflé by pulling it against the back of a knife. Spread the chocolate cream over the top of the soufflé and mark it roughly with a palette knife.
10 Sprinkle chocolate curls or grated chocolate over the top of the chocolate cream and press some onto the exposed edges of the soufflé.
11 Pipe rosettes from the reserved cream around the top edge of the soufflé. Decorate with small leaves if desired. Keep refrigerated until serving.

Poached Pears with Strawberry Sauce (above); Chocolate Soufflé (above); Hazelnut Pastry Gâteau (page 100)

Cook's note: *A cold soufflé looks insignificant if it is not set about 2·5cm (1in) above the rim of the dish. Do check that the top diameter of the soufflé dish is no more than 15cm (6in) and ensure that it is no more than 6·5cm (2¾in) in height*

for the sponge base:
2 eggs, size 2
50g (2oz) caster sugar
50g (2oz) plain flour
a pinch of salt
¼ × 5ml tsp (¼tsp) baking
   powder
25g (1oz) butter, melted and
   cooled

for the topping:
135g (4¼oz) packet lemon jelly
   (three-quarters only required)
cold water
3 eggs, size 2, separated
100g (4oz) caster sugar
2 lemons, finely grated rind and
   strained juice
1 envelope of gelatin
150ml (¼pt) double cream
for decoration: whipped cream
   and thin slices of fresh
   lemon, optional

Lemon slices (*serves 8*)   colour page 99
POWER LEVEL: 100% (FULL)

1 Line the base of a shallow 22cm (8½in) square flexible plastic microwave dish with greaseproof paper. (The use of a flexible dish is important when finally loosening the dessert from the dish.) Lightly grease the paper.
2 Whisk the eggs and caster sugar together until they are very thick and will hold a trail for at least 5 sec.
3 Gently sift the flour, salt and baking powder over the surface of the whisked mixture, then carefully fold in. Gradually fold in the melted butter.
4 Pour the sponge mixture into the prepared dish. Cook for 2–2½ min until well risen and springy to the touch, but very slightly moist on the top. Allow to stand for 1 min, then turn onto a cooling rack to cool. Set the sponge aside. Wash and dry the dish as it is needed for the topping.
5 Put three-quarters of the packet jelly into a small mixing bowl (the rest is not needed) and heat for 45 sec until the jelly melts. Make the jelly up to 275ml (½pt) with chilled water and stir well. Pour the jelly into the clean dish, then refrigerate until the jelly sets. (The jelly will set more quickly if placed in the freezing compartment for a short time.)
6 Meanwhile, whisk the egg yolks with the caster sugar and lemon rind until very thick. Gradually whisk in the lemon juice.
7 Put 3 × 15ml tbsp (3tbsp) cold water into a small mixing bowl, sprinkle the gelatin over the top and leave to stand for about 1 min until the gelatin swells and turns opaque.
8 Whisk the cream until it will just hold soft peaks. Whisk the egg whites until stiff. Heat the gelatin for 30–40 sec until it is melted and very hot.
9 Whisk the gelatin into the lemon mixture, then fold in the cream. Quickly fold in the egg whites. Pour the mixture on top of the set jelly, then refrigerate for about 2 hr until quite set.
10 When the lemon mousse mixture is set, place the sponge square on the top.
11 To unmould: loosen the sides of the mousse from the dish with a knife. Place a flat board on top of the sponge, invert the board and the dish together. Place a hot teatowel on top of the dish to loosen the jelly. Carefully remove the dish. If the jelly is difficult to unmould, dip the base of the dish into hot water for a few seconds.
12 Trim the edges of the mousse mixture to neaten and line up with the sponge base. Cut into 8 equal-sized pieces. Decorate each slice with whipped cream and lemon slices if desired. Keep refrigerated until serving.

DO NOT FREEZE

175g (6oz) plain flour
a pinch of salt
25g (1oz) caster sugar
75g (3oz) butter
2 egg yolks, size 2
2 × 5ml tsp (2tsp) cold water

Sweet pastry flan case (*makes 1 × 24cm/9½in flan case*)
POWER LEVEL: 100% (FULL)

1 Sift the flour, salt and sugar into a mixing bowl, rub in the butter until the mixture resembles fine breadcrumbs. Mix the egg yolks and cold water together, pour into the rubbed-in mixture and mix lightly together to bind.
2 Lightly knead the pastry on a lightly floured board until smooth. Roll out to a round large enough to line a 24cm (9½in) flan dish.
3 Carefully fit the pastry into the dish, pressing it well into the base and up the sides. Trim and decorate the edge. Prick well, all over the base and sides, with a fork. Shield the upright edges with a smooth strip of foil and line the pastry case with kitchen paper.
4 Cook for 4½–5 min. Remove the foil and paper and continue to cook for a further 1½–2 min until evenly cooked all over.

Apple and orange flan *(serves 8)*

POWER LEVEL: 100% (FULL)

1 Wash, peel, quarter, core and slice the apples. Put the slices into a large heat-resistant mixing bowl, add the orange rind and granulated sugar and mix lightly together.
2 Cover the bowl with clingfilm, pulling it back by about a quarter to allow for venting and stirring. Cook the apples for 15–20 min, stirring every 5 min, until the apples are soft and fluffy.
3 Pour the cooked apples into a large nylon sieve, placed over a mixing bowl and allow to drain well until cooled.
4 Put the marmalade into a small heat-resistant bowl, and heat for 1–2 min until melted and boiling.
5 Brush the inside of the flan case with a little of the boiling marmalade. Stir 1 × 15ml tbsp (1tbsp) of the grand marnier into the rest.
6 Fill the flan case with the well-drained apples and smooth the surface (the juice will not be needed). Spoon the remaining marmalade evenly over the apples to glaze. Chill well.
7 Whisk the cream with the remaining grand marnier and caster sugar until thick but not buttery. Spoon into a large piping bag fitted with a large star nozzle. Pipe a decorative border around the edge of the apple flan, leaving the centre clear.

24cm (9½in) cooked sweet pastry flan case, left in dish (page 00)

for the filling:
1½kg (3lb) cooking apples
finely grated rind of 2 large oranges
225g (8oz) granulated sugar
3 heaped 15ml tbsp (3 heaped tbsp) fine-shred marmalade
2 × 15ml tbsp (2tbsp) grand marnier, optional
225ml (8fl oz) double cream
1 × 5ml tsp (1tsp) caster sugar

Caribbean bananas *(serves 4)*

POWER LEVEL: 100% (FULL)

1 Beat the cream cheese with the sugar until soft, then beat in the double cream, vanilla and cinnamon.
2 Put the butter and rum into a shallow heat-resistant dish, large enough to take the bananas in a single layer. Heat for 1 min. Add the bananas, turning them in the butter and rum to coat. Cook for 2 min, turning and repositioning the bananas after 1 min.
3 Pour the cheese mixture over the bananas, then sprinkle with freshly grated nutmeg. Cook for 3 min, repositioning and turning the bananas after 1½ min. Allow to stand for 1 min before serving. Serve hot.

DO NOT FREEZE

100g (4oz) cream cheese
50g (2oz) soft light brown sugar
150ml (¼pt) double cream
½ × 5ml tsp (½tsp) vanilla essence
½ × 5ml tsp (½tsp) ground cinnamon
25g (1oz) unsalted butter
2 × 15ml tbsp (2tbsp) rum
4 large ripe but firm bananas, peeled
freshly grated nutmeg

Cakes, breads and pastries

If a microwave-baked cake stales quickly, it is an indication that it has been slightly overcooked, or that the mixture was a little too dry before cooking. One way of overcoming the problem is to wrap the cake as soon as possible after cooking to prevent extra moisture loss, leaving it to cool in the wrapping before icing and decorating. If the cake is particularly light and moist and difficult to handle while still hot, make a tent of foil or cover loosely with clingfilm over the cake on the cooling rack.

Some cakes, breads and pastries may benefit by cooking on a baking rack or trivet in the microwave to allow more efficient penetration of the microwave energy to the base of the cake. It is not always necessary, but worth remembering if required.

Coffee praline ring (*serves 8*) *colour opposite*
POWER LEVEL: 70%
CONVENTIONAL HOTPLATE

for the sponge:
100g (4oz) unsalted butter
100g (4oz) caster sugar
1 × 15ml tbsp (1tbsp) strong
    black coffee
2 eggs, size 2
100g (4oz) self-raising flour

for the praline:
oil
50g (2oz) whole unblanched
    almonds
50g (2oz) granulated sugar

for the butter cream:
100g (4oz) unsalted butter
2 egg whites
100g (4oz) caster sugar
2 × 15ml tbsp (2tbsp) strong
    black coffee

1 Lightly butter a 20cm (8in) ring mould.
2 To make the sponge: beat the butter and caster sugar together until very light and fluffy, then beat in the coffee. Beat in the eggs, one at a time, beating well between each addition. Carefully fold in the flour.
3 Spoon the sponge mixture into the prepared mould and spread evenly. Cook for 5½–7 min until well risen and firm to the touch, yet slightly moist on the top. Allow the sponge to cool in the mould for a few minutes, then turn it out onto a rack to cool.
4 To make the praline: lightly oil a small baking sheet. Put the almonds and sugar into a small, heavy-based saucepan. Heat very gently on a conventional hotplate, shaking the pan from time to time, until the sugar dissolves and turns a rich golden brown. Pour the praline immediately onto the greased baking sheet.
5 When the praline is quite cold, put it into a very strong polythene bag and crush finely with a mallet or rolling pin.
6 To make the butter cream: beat the butter until it is very soft and creamy. Put the egg whites and the caster sugar into a mixing bowl, then place the bowl over a pan of gently simmering water. Whisk the whites until a stiff shiny meringue is formed. Alternatively, whisk in a food mixer using maximum setting.
7 Gradually beat the meringue into the butter, a spoonful at a time, then beat in the coffee to taste.
8 Cut the sponge into 3 even-sized layers, cutting horizontally. Sandwich the layers together with just a little of the butter cream.
9 Put 2 × 15ml tbsp (2tbsp) of the butter cream into a piping bag fitted with a medium-sized star nozzle. Spread the remaining cream in a thin layer all over the sponge, then sprinkle the praline evenly all over the butter cream.
10 Place the cake on a flat serving plate, then pipe a decorative border around the bottom edge.

Coffee Praline Ring (above); Lemon Slices (page 96)

for the pastry:
175g (6oz) plain flour
pinch salt
50g (2oz) caster sugar
50g (2oz) ground, toasted
   hazelnuts
175g (6oz) unsalted butter
flour
25g (1oz) chopped, toasted
   hazelnuts

for the filling:
425ml (¾pt) double cream
1 × 15ml tbsp (1tbsp) caster
   sugar
1 × 5ml tsp (1tsp) vanilla
   essence
350g (12oz) fresh strawberries,
   hulled
icing sugar for sifting

Hazelnut pastry gâteau *(serves 8)*   *colour page 99*
POWER LEVEL: 100% (FULL)

1 Lightly butter a 24cm (9½in) flan dish, and line the base with a round of non-stick baking paper or lightly greased greaseproof paper.

2 To make the pastry: sift the flour, salt and sugar into a mixing bowl, then mix in the ground hazelnuts. Rub the butter into the flour, and gently press the mixture together to form a ball.

3 Cut the pastry into 2 equal pieces. Roll out 1 piece on a very lightly floured surface to a round about 15cm (6in) diameter. Place the round of pastry in the lined flan dish, then press it out gently with a floured hand until it fits the dish exactly. Smooth the pastry with a spoon.

4 Cook the pastry for 4–5 min until the pastry is cooked. Allow to cool for a few minutes in the dish, then loosen the sides with a knife and very carefully turn the pastry out onto a rack to cool.

5 Wash and reline the dish. Roll out the remaining piece of pastry and fit into the dish as above and sprinkle with the chopped hazelnuts, pressing the nuts very lightly into the pastry. Cook as above.

6 Cool the cooked pastry for a few minutes, then turn out very carefully onto a rack. While it is still warm, cut it into 8 equal triangles. Cool completely.

7 Whisk the cream with the sugar and the vanilla essence until it is thick but not buttery. Put 2 × 15ml tbsp (2tbsp) of the cream into a piping bag fitted with a large star nozzle.

8 Place the solid round of pastry on a large flat serving plate, and spread with half of the remaining cream.

9 Put 8 small strawberries (or 8 halves if they are large) aside for decoration. Cut the rest into halves (or quarters) and arrange them over the cream spread on the pastry round. Spread the rest of the cream over the strawberries.

10 Lift alternate triangles from the cut pastry round, and place them in exactly the same position on top of the cream. Sift the remaining 4 triangles with icing sugar, then place these in position on top of the cream.

11 Pipe a whirl of cream on each triangle of pastry, then decorate with the reserved strawberries.

Cook's note: *When preparing and lining the flan dish, leave a paper 'handle' on each side to enable the pastry round to be lifted more easily from the dish*

Pistachio and pear gâteau (serves 6–8)
POWER LEVEL: 100% (FULL)

1   Lightly butter an oblong microwave dish, about 24 × 15 × 6cm (9½ × 6 × 2½in), and line the bottom with a piece of non-stick baking paper.
2   To make the sponge: whisk the eggs and sugar together until they are very thick and creamy, and will hold a trail for at least 5 sec. Sift the plain flour, cornflour, baking powder and pistachio nuts into the whisked mixture, then fold in very gently. Carefully fold in the melted butter.
3   Pour the sponge mixture into the prepared dish. Cook for 2½–3 min, until well risen and firm to the touch, but still slightly moist on the top. Allow the sponge to cool in the dish for a few minutes then turn it out onto a rack to cool.
4   Whisk the cream with the kirsch and sugar until it is thick but not buttery. Put 2–3 × 15ml tbsp (2–3tbsp) of the cream into a piping bag fitted with a small star nozzle.
5   Cut the pears into thin slices.
6   Cut the sponge cake in half horizontally. Spread the bottom half with some of the cream, then arrange the pears on top. Place the other half of the sponge on top of the pears.
7   Spread cream around the sides of the sponge, then coat them evenly with toasted hazelnuts or almonds. Spread more cream evenly over the top of the cake.
8   Pipe a decorative border of cream around the top edge of the sponge, then pipe diagonal rows of cream on the top, spacing them about 2·5cm (1in) apart. Sprinkle the ground pistachio nuts over the cream.

for the sponge:
3 eggs, size 2
75g (3oz) caster sugar
65g (2½oz) plain flour
15g (½oz) cornflour
½ × 5ml tsp (½tsp) baking powder
25g (1oz) pistachio nuts, skinned and finely ground
40g (1½oz) butter, melted and cooled

for the filling:
275ml (½pt) double cream
2 × 15ml tbsp (2tbsp) kirsch
25g (1oz) caster sugar
425g (15oz) can pear halves, well drained
75g (3oz) chopped toasted hazelnuts, or almonds
15g (½oz) ground pistachio nuts

Charentais flan (serves 8)
POWER LEVEL: 100% (FULL)

1   Cut each melon in half and scoop out the seeds into a sieve placed over a bowl. Allow the juice to drain into the bowl.
2   Remove 12 small balls from the melon flesh, with a melon baller or a small teaspoon. Put these into a small bowl, cover with clingfilm and refrigerate until required.
3   Scoop out all the flesh from the melons and purée it in a food processor or blender – there should be about 550ml (1pt) melon purée.
4   Put the purée into a mixing bowl, then stir in the orange rind and juice, caster sugar and the juice drained from the seeds. Stir until the sugar dissolves.
5   Pour the cold water into a small bowl and sprinkle the gelatin evenly over the top. Allow to stand for a few minutes until the gelatin swells and turns opaque.
6   Heat the gelatin for about 30 sec until it dissolves and becomes very hot. Quickly whisk the gelatin into the melon purée.
7   Whisk 125ml (4fl oz) of the cream until it will hold soft peaks, then gradually stir in the melon purée. Chill the melon mixture until it is almost on the point of setting, stirring from time to time to prevent separation.
8   Heat the apricot jam for about 1 min until it is boiling hot. Brush the inside of the flan case with the apricot jam, then carefully pour in the setting melon mixture. Refrigerate the flan for at least 3 hr until thoroughly set.
9   Whisk the remaining cream until it is thick but not buttery. Decorate the flan with piped cream, and the reserved melon balls. Keep the flan refrigerated until serving.

2 × 675g (1½lb) very ripe charentais melons
very finely grated rind and strained juice of 1 large orange
50g (2oz) caster sugar
75ml (3fl oz) cold water
2 envelopes of gelatin
275ml (½pt) double cream
2 × 15ml tbsp (2tbsp) apricot jam, sieved
24cm (9½in) cooked, sweet pastry, flan case (page 96), left in the dish

DO NOT FREEZE

450g (1lb) strong plain flour
150g (5oz) caster sugar
½ × 5ml tsp (½tsp) salt
50g (2oz) butter
1 sachet easy-blend yeast
finely grated rind of 1 orange
225ml (8fl oz) tepid milk
1 egg, size 2, beaten
2 × 5ml tsp (2tsp) mixed spice
40g (1½oz) glacé cherries,
    chopped
40g (1½oz) cut mixed peel
40g (1½oz) glacé pineapple,
    chopped
40g (1½oz) angelica, chopped
50g (2oz) butter, melted

Spicy rings (*makes 2*)   *colour opposite*
POWER LEVEL: 100% (FULL)

1   Sift the flour, 25g (1oz) of the sugar and the salt into a mixing bowl, then rub in the butter. Add the yeast and orange rind and mix well together.
2   Make a well in the centre of the flour, add the milk and egg, then mix well to form a dough. Knead the dough on a lightly floured surface for about 10 min until it is smooth and elastic.
3   Put the dough into a clean bowl and cover with clingfilm. Prove the dough by placing the bowl in the microwave and heating for 15 sec then leaving for 10 min, repeating until the dough has doubled in size.
4   Turn the risen dough onto a lightly floured surface, then knead again for 2–3 min to expel the air bubbles. Cut the dough into 36 small pieces and shape each piece into a neat ball.
5   Mix the remaining caster sugar and spice together. Mix the cherries, peel, pineapple and angelica together.
6   Butter two 20cm (8in), deep ring moulds.
7   Dip each dough ball in the melted butter, then roll them in the sugar and spice mixture.
8   Sprinkle a little of the fruit mixture in the bottom of each mould, then add a layer of dough balls, spacing them well apart. Continue to layer up fruit mixture and dough balls, using 18 balls for each mould.
9   Cover the moulds loosely with clingfilm and prove, one at a time, as in step 3, until the dough has doubled in size. Remove the clingfilm and cook for 4½–5 min until well risen, firm and springy to the touch.
10 Allow to cool in the moulds for a few minutes, then turn out onto a rack to cool.

450g (1lb) strong plain flour
50g (2oz) caster sugar
½ × 5ml tsp (½tsp) salt
75g (3oz) butter
finely grated rind of 1 lemon
1 sachet easy-blend yeast
225ml (8fl oz) soured cream
1 egg, size 2, beaten
50g (2oz) raisins
50g (2oz) sultanas
50g (2oz) cut mixed peel

for the topping:
2 × 15ml tbsp (2tbsp) apricot
    jam, sieved
15g (½oz) flaked almonds,
    toasted
1 × 15ml tbsp (1tbsp) crushed
    sugar cubes
1 × 15ml tbsp (1tbsp) cut
    mixed peel

Advent ring (*serves 8*)   *colour opposite*
POWER LEVEL: 100% (FULL)
CONVENTIONAL GRILL

1   Sift the flour, sugar and salt into a mixing bowl, then rub in the butter. Add the lemon rind and yeast and mix well together.
2   Make a well in the centre of the flour, add the soured cream and egg, and mix together to form a dough. Knead the dough on a lightly floured surface for 10 min until it is very smooth and elastic.
3   Put the dough into a clean bowl and cover with clingfilm. Prove the dough by placing the bowl in the microwave and heating for 15 sec then leaving for 10 min, repeating until the dough has doubled in size.
4   Butter a 30cm (12in), deep, heatproof ring mould, or butter a 30cm (12in) heatproof flan dish and the outside of a wide tumbler. Place the tumbler in the centre of the flan dish.
5   Turn the risen dough onto a very lightly floured surface and knead for 2–3 min to knock out the air bubbles. Knead in the raisins, sultanas and cut mixed peel.
6   Cut the dough into 3 equal pieces. Shape each piece into a long roll about 45·5cm (18in) long. Plait the rolls neatly together, then join the ends together to form a ring.
7   Place the plaited ring in the buttered ring mould, or around the glass in the flan dish.
8   Cover the plait with clingfilm, then prove, as in step 3, until the dough has doubled in size. Remove the clingfilm and cook for 5–6 min until well risen and firm and springy to the touch.
9   If used, remove the tumbler from the flan dish and brown the top of the plait under a hot grill. Allow to cool in the dish for a few minutes, then turn out carefully onto a rack to cool.

Spicy Rings (above); Advent Ring (above)

10 Heat the jam for 1–2 min until it is boiling hot. Brush the jam over the plait, then sprinkle with the flaked almonds, crushed sugar cubes and the cut mixed peel.
11 To serve, place the plait on a large napkin- or doily-lined plate, then place a large candle in the centre.

Cook's note: *If the dish used for baking is not suitable for placing under the grill, carefully remove the plait from the dish and place upright onto a wire grid or heatproof plate before browning the top under the grill. Leave to cool*

1 × 5ml tsp (1tsp) sugar
150ml (¼pt) water, approximately
2 × 5ml tsp (2tsp) dried yeast
225g (8oz) plain flour
½ × 5ml tsp (½tsp) salt
50g (2oz) butter or margarine
2 eggs, size 3, beaten
25g (1oz) flaked almonds

for the syrup:
100g (4oz) caster sugar
150ml (¼pt) water
1 × 5ml tsp (1tsp) lemon juice
2 × 15ml tbsp (2tbsp) kirsch
for serving: toasted almonds, fruit to choice and cream

Savarin *(serves 8)*   *colour page 59*
POWER LEVEL: 100% (FULL)
CONVENTIONAL OVEN TEMPERATURE: 200°C (400°F) MARK 6

1 Lightly grease a 20cm (8in) heatproof microwave ring mould.
2 Add the sugar to the water and warm for 30 sec. Stir in the yeast and leave for 8–12 min to activate.
3 Sift the flour and salt and warm for 15 sec. Add the yeast mixture and a little more water if necessary. Mix and knead the dough well until soft.
4 Cover and prove by heating for 10 sec and leaving for 5 min. Repeat until double in size.
5 Melt the butter or margarine for 1½ min. Beat the butter and eggs into the dough until it resembles a thick batter. Beat well.
6 Arrange the flaked almonds in the base of the container and carefully pour in the batter.
7 Cover with clingfilm and prove as in step 4, until the mixture is well risen in the mould.
8 Remove the clingfilm and cook the savarin in a preheated oven for about 40 min until well risen and golden brown. Turn out onto a rack.
9 Prepare the syrup: add the sugar to the water and heat for 1 min. Stir until the sugar is dissolved. Bring to the boil in the microwave and keep boiling until a thick syrup is formed.
10 Stir in the lemon juice and kirsch and pour over the savarin while warm.
11 Decorate the top of the savarin with toasted almonds and fill the centre with fruit to choice. Serve with cream.

450g (1lb) strong plain flour
25g (1oz) caster sugar
½ × 5ml tsp (½tsp) salt
50g (2oz) butter
1 sachet easy-blend yeast
200ml (7fl oz) tepid milk
25ml (1fl oz) rum
1 egg, size 2, beaten
175g (6oz) ready to eat prunes, roughly chopped
icing sugar for sifting

Prune bread *(makes 2 loaves)*
POWER LEVEL: 100% (FULL)

1 Sift the flour, sugar and salt into a mixing bowl, then rub in the butter. Add the yeast and mix thoroughly together.
2 Make a well in the centre of the flour and add the milk, rum and egg. Mix together to form a dough. Knead the dough on a lightly floured surface for 10 min until very smooth and elastic.
3 Put the dough into a clean bowl and cover with clingfilm. Prove the dough by placing the bowl in the microwave and heating for 15 sec then leaving for 10 min, repeating until the dough has doubled in size.
4 Turn the risen dough onto a lightly floured surface and knead once again for 2–3 min to expel the air bubbles. Knead the prunes into the dough.
5 Cut the dough into 2 equal pieces, then shape each one neatly and place in a small, buttered loaf mould.
6 Loosely cover the loaf moulds with clingfilm and prove, one at a time as in step 3, until the dough has doubled in size. Remove the clingfilm and cook for 3½–4 min until well risen, firm and springy to the touch.
7 Allow the loaves to cool for a few minutes, then turn out onto a rack to cool. Dredge heavily with icing sugar when cold. Serve sliced and buttered.

Upside-down peach tart *(serves 6)*
POWER LEVEL: 100% (FULL)

8 medium-sized fresh peaches
boiling water
75g (3oz) caster sugar
½ bottle red wine

for the pastry:
50g (2oz) plain flour
50g (2oz) self-raising flour
pinch salt
1 × 15ml tbsp (1tbsp) caster
   sugar
50g (2oz) unsalted butter
finely grated rind of 1 lemon
1 egg yolk, mixed with 2 × 5ml
   tsp (2tsp) cold water
for serving: ice cream or cream

1 Cut each peach in half and remove the stone. Place the peach halves in a large bowl and cover with boiling water. Leave to stand for 1–2 min, then remove from the water. Remove the skin from the peach halves.
2 Place the peach halves, rounded sides down, in a 24cm (9½in) flan dish, sprinkle with caster sugar and carefully pour over the wine. Cover the dish with clingfilm, pulling back 1 edge to vent. Cook for 6–8 min, until tender.
3 Place a plate on top of the flan dish, then strain the wine from the peaches into a small bowl. Bring the wine to the boil in the microwave, then boil, uncovered, until it reduces and becomes very syrupy. Pour back over the peaches and allow to cool.
4 To make the pastry: sift the flours, salt and sugar into a mixing bowl, then rub in the butter until the mixture resembles fine breadcrumbs. Stir in the lemon rind and mix to a firm dough with the egg yolk.
5 Roll the pastry out on a lightly floured surface to a round, 12mm (½in) larger than the flan dish, and fold the edge of the pastry in by 12mm (½in).
6 Prick the pastry well with a fork, then place it, folded side down, on top of the peaches and wine. Cook for 12 min, until the pastry is cooked. Allow to cool in the dish, then very carefully turn the tart out onto a large serving plate. Serve warm with ice cream or cream.

Rum babas *(makes 9)*
POWER LEVEL: 100% (FULL)

225g (8oz) strong plain flour
½ × 5ml tsp (½tsp) salt
50g (2oz) caster sugar
1 sachet easy-blend yeast
4 × 15ml tbsp (4tbsp) milk
4 eggs, size 2, beaten
175g (6oz) unsalted butter,
   softened
butter

for the syrup:
450g (1lb) granulated sugar
550ml (1pt) water
150ml (¼pt) rum

for the glaze:
4 × 15ml tbsp (4tbsp) apricot
   jam, sieved

for the filling:
425ml (¾pt) double cream
2 kiwi fruits, peeled and sliced
23 black grapes, halved and
   pips removed
18 white grapes, halved and
   pips removed

1 To make the babas: put the flour, salt and sugar into a mixing bowl, add the yeast and mix well. Make a well in the centre, and add the milk and eggs. Beat well for about 10 min until the dough becomes very elasticated.
2 Cover the bowl with clingfilm, and rise the dough by placing the bowl in the microwave and heating for 15 sec then leaving for 10 min, repeating until the dough has doubled in size.
3 Gradually beat the butter, a little at a time, into the risen dough, beating well between each addition.
4 Lightly butter nine 150ml (¼pt) individual soufflé dishes. If you do not have so many dishes, rise and cook the babas in batches.
5 Half fill each soufflé dish with the yeast mixture. Place 6 dishes in a circle, evenly spaced, in the microwave and loosely cover with clingfilm. Prove, as in step 2, until the dough reaches the top of the moulds.
6 Remove the clingfilm and cook for 3½–4 min, until firm and springy to the touch, taking care not to overcook. Prove the remaining dough in the same way, cooking the 3 babas for 1½–2 min. Turn the babas onto a rack.
7 To make the syrup: put the sugar and water into a large bowl, and heat gently until every granule of sugar dissolves. Bring to the boil in the microwave, and boil for 2 min. Stir in the rum.
8 Dip the babas in the hot syrup until they absorb it, turning them over if they are not completely immersed. Carefully lift from the syrup and place on a cooling rack, placing the rack over a tray to catch the drips.
9 Heat the jam for about 2 min until it is boiling hot. Brush the jam over each baba to glaze evenly.
10 Whisk the cream until it is thick but not buttery. Spoon into a large piping bag fitted with a medium-sized star nozzle.
11 Split each baba diagonally from one top edge almost down to the opposite side. Gently ease the babas open and fill them with whipped cream, kiwi fruit and grapes, reserving a few grapes for decoration.
12 Pipe a whirl of cream on each baba, then decorate with the reserved grapes.

450g (1lb) strong plain flour
½ × 5ml tsp (½tsp) salt
50g (2oz) caster sugar
1 sachet easy-blend yeast
5 eggs, size 2, beaten
6 × 15ml tbsp (6tbsp) milk
225g (8oz) butter, softened

Brioche (*makes two 17·5cm (7in) brioches*)
POWER LEVEL: 100% (FULL)
CONVENTIONAL GRILL

1 Sift the flour, salt and caster sugar into a large mixing bowl, add the yeast and mix thoroughly together.
2 Make a well in the centre of the flour, then pour in the eggs and the milk, mix together to make a very soft dough. Beat the dough for about 10 min until it becomes very elasticated. (This can be done in an electric mixer, using the beating attachment.)
3 Gradually beat the softened butter into the dough, adding a little at a time, and beating well after each addition until the butter is absorbed before adding the next.
4 Cover the bowl of dough with clingfilm, then refrigerate overnight.
5 Next day, remove the dough from the refrigerator and divide it into two equal pieces. Shape each piece into a neat round on a floured surface, then place each one in a buttered, deep 7·5cm (7in) fluted or plain heat-proof glass mould, or soufflé dish.
6 Cover the dishes loosely with clingfilm. Place 1 loaf at a time in the microwave and prove by heating for 15 sec then leaving to stand for 10 min, repeating until the dough has doubled in size.
7 Remove the clingfilm and cook for 4 min until the loaf is well risen and firm and springy to the touch. Brown the top under a hot grill. Allow to cool in the dish for a few minutes, then turn out onto a rack to cool.

450g (1lb) strong plain flour
50g (2oz) caster sugar
½ × 5ml tsp (½tsp) salt
50g (2oz) butter
1 sachet easy-blend yeast
150ml (¼pt) tepid milk
2 eggs, size 2, beaten
25g (1oz) butter, melted
100g (4oz) plain chocolate, finely chopped
225g (8oz) icing sugar, sieved
2 × 15ml tbsp (2tbsp) boiling water
15g (½oz) plain chocolate, grated

Iced pain au chocolat (*makes 2*)
POWER LEVEL: 100% (FULL)

1 Sift the flour, sugar and salt into a mixing bowl, then rub the butter into the flour. Add the yeast and mix thoroughly together.
2 Make a well in the centre of the flour, add the milk and eggs, then mix well together to form a dough. Knead the dough on a lightly floured surface for 10 min until smooth and elastic.
3 Place the dough in a clean bowl and cover with clingfilm. Prove the dough by placing the bowl in the microwave and heating for 15 sec then leaving for 10 min, repeating until the dough has doubled in size.
4 Turn the risen dough onto a lightly floured surface and knead once again for 2–3 min to expel the air bubbles. Roll the dough out to a rectangle 40 × 30cm (16 × 12in).
5 Brush the dough with melted butter, then sprinkle evenly with the chopped chocolate. Roll the dough up, from the longest side, to form a roll. Cut the roll into sixteen 2·5cm (1in) pieces.
6 Butter two 22·5cm (9in) flan dishes. Place 1 slice of the dough, cut side up, in the centre of each dish. Arrange 7 slices of dough around each centre piece, cut side up, and with the joins to the centre.
7 Loosely cover each dish with clingfilm, and prove one at a time as in step 3, until the dough has doubled in size. Remove the clingfilm and cook for 3 min until well risen, springy and firm to the touch. Cool in the dish for a few minutes, then carefully turn out onto a cooling rack.
8 Mix the icing sugar and boiling water together to form a fairly thick, runny icing. Dribble the glacé icing from side to side over the warm pain au chocolat to form lines. Sprinkle immediately with the grated chocolate. Leave to cool and set.

Tipsy Chestnut Gâteau (page 93);
Baked Salmon with Hazelnut
Stuffing (page 32)

Menus for entertaining

MENU FOR 4

Iced borsch

★　　　★　　　★

Salmon trout in aspic
Green salad
Celeriac salad with walnuts

★　　　★　　　★

Crêpes suzette

The following timetable is a guide to the order of preparation and cooking for serving dinner at 8.30 pm, but can be easily adapted for a lunch-time meal if required.

Day before
Make the iced borsch, cover and chill in the refrigerator.
Make the aspic jelly and the mayonnaise.
Make the pancakes, keep 8–12 in the refrigerator for serving at the meal and freeze the remainder for another time.

Morning or afternoon
Prepare the salad vegetables.
Prepare the garnishes for the salmon and salads.
Cook the salmon and leave to cool. Melt the jelly in the microwave and coat the salmon and garnishes. Reserve any remaining aspic jelly for garnishing the dish later. Refrigerate the salmon until required.
Assemble all the equipment and ingredients ready for the final preparation from about 7·30 pm.

Order of cooking
7.30　Fill and fold the pancakes ready for reheating later.
7.50　Assemble the salads ready for serving.
8.05　Chop the reserved aspic jelly and use to garnish around the salmon.
8.20　Add the orange juice to the borsch and garnish with orange.
8.30　Serve the first course.

After the main course, reheat the pancakes and heat the rum. Flame at the table with the hot rum and serve.

1 onion, chopped
1 carrot, chopped
675g (1½lb) raw beetroot, diced
2–3 sprigs parsley
1 bay leaf
1 bouquet garni
salt and freshly ground black pepper
1 litre (1¾pt) boiling chicken stock (page 20)
2 × 5ml tsp (2tsp) sugar
1 × 15ml tbsp (1tbsp) orange juice
for garnish: slices of orange

Iced borsch
POWER LEVEL: 100% (FULL) AND 50%

1　Place all the ingredients except the orange juice into a large bowl or dish.
2　Cover the bowl or dish and bring to the boil in the microwave on 100% (full) setting. Uncover the bowl and cook for 15 min. Reduce to 50% setting and cook for a further 15–20 min until the beetroot is tender.
3　Strain the soup through a fine sieve or muslin cloth. Adjust the seasoning, leave to cool and then chill in the refrigerator.
4　Just before serving, stir in the orange juice and garnish with slices of orange.

Salmon trout in aspic   *colour page 111*
POWER LEVEL: 100% (FULL) AND 70%

This dish also makes an excellent centrepiece for a formal buffet, and in addition may be served as a starter. A large pink trout or small salmon can be cooked and served in the same way

1   Clean the fish, the head and tail may be removed if preferred, depending on the size and length of the fish. Wash and pat dry with kitchen paper towel.
2   Sprinkle with salt and pepper and place the bay leaves inside the fish. Place the fish on a sheet of greaseproof paper.
3   Melt the butter for 1 min in a bowl and use this to coat the salmon trout thoroughly. Sprinkle with the lemon juice. Protect the thin ends, ie the head and tail, with small pieces of aluminium foil. Wrap the fish tightly in the greaseproof paper and place on the microwave cooker shelf.
4   Reduce to 70% setting and cook for 10–12 min, turning the fish over and around once halfway through. Leave to cool slightly then refrigerate until cold.
5   Remove the bay leaves, and skin the fish, leaving on the head and tail. Place onto a cooling tray with a large plate underneath.
6   Make the aspic jelly and when it is beginning to thicken, coat the top of the fish thinly. Leave to set.
7   Decorate the fish, using thin rings of radish and olives, diamonds or strips of tomato skins and lemon rind, thin cucumber slices or strips of skin, parsley sprigs and peeled shrimps or prawns.
8   Coat with another layer of aspic jelly, allow to set and add more layers, leaving to set in between, until the decorations are held in place. Carefully transfer the fish to a serving platter and chill.
9   Leave any dripping of aspic jelly on the plate beneath to set, then chop with a sharp knife and use as a garnish around the salmon trout. Serve with a mixed salad and mayonnaise.

DO NOT FREEZE

1 salmon trout, 900g (2lb) approximately
salt and pepper
2 bay leaves
25g (1oz) butter
juice ½ lemon
425ml (¾pt) aspic jelly (page 109)
for garnish: radishes, stuffed olives, tomato skins, pared lemon rind, cucumber, parsley, shrimps or prawns
for serving: mixed salad and mayonnaise (page 76)

Aspic jelly
POWER LEVEL: 100% (FULL)

In order to achieve a perfectly clear stock you will need to ensure that all utensils and cloths used for this recipe are well scalded in boiling water. You will require 3 large bowls, 1 small bowl or jug, a whisk, metal spoon and a teatowel

1   Place the stock into a large bowl, cover and heat for 4–5 min until warm. Whisk the egg whites to a light froth and whisk them into the stock.
2   Heat the wine and sherry for 2–3 min, add the gelatin and stir well. If the gelatin is not completely dissolved heat for a further 30–45 sec and stir again.
3   Whisk the gelatin into the stock and heat for 6–8 min, stirring, every minute until almost boiling.
4   Heat for 4–5 min, or until boiling rapidly, without stirring. Stand for 5 min. Repeat this process twice more.
5   After the third standing period, strain the aspic through a scalded teacloth into a bowl. Strain the aspic again through the cloth into another scalded bowl. Allow to cool and use as required.

Cook's note: *At first glance, you may not think it is worth the trouble of making your own aspic jelly, but the flavour is excellent and far better than commercial varieties available*

DO NOT FREEZE

1 litre (1¾pt) chicken, meat or fish stock (page 20), skimmed and free of grease
2 egg whites
150ml (¼pt) dry white wine and dry sherry mixed
50g (2oz) gelatin

1 celeriac, peeled
3 × 15ml tbsp (3tbsp) salted
    water
2 × 15ml tbsp (2tbsp)
    mayonnaise (page 76)
2 × 15ml tbsp (2tbsp) soured
    cream
2 × 15ml tbsp (2tbsp) finely
    chopped walnuts
1 × 15ml tbsp (1tbsp) chopped
    chives or parsley

Celeriac salad with walnuts
POWER LEVEL: 100% (FULL)

1 Cut the peeled celeriac into julienne strips or matchstick-sized pieces.
   Place in a dish with the salted water, cover and cook for 3–4 min until
   the celeriac is just blanched. Toss over the the celeriac once halfway
   through cooking.
2 Drain and refresh the celeriac in cold water and leave to cool. Beat together
   the mayonnaise and soured cream and fold in the walnuts.
3 Combine the celeriac with the dressing. Sprinkle with the chopped chives
   or parsley and serve cold with fresh salmon, slices of raw smoked ham or
   salmon, or thin slices of salami.

DO NOT FREEZE

for the batter:
150g (5oz) plain flour
a pinch of salt
25g (1oz) caster sugar
2 eggs, size 2
40g (1½oz) butter, melted
2 × 5ml tsp (2tsp) brandy, or
    rum
finely grated rind of 1 orange
350ml (12fl oz) milk
a little butter for cooking

for the filling:
75g (3oz) butter
75g (3oz) caster sugar
finely grated rind of 1 large
    orange and 4 × 15ml tbsp
    (4tbsp) juice, strained
2 × 15ml tbsp (2tbsp) orange
    curaçao or grand marnier
3 × 15ml tbsp (3tbsp) rum
for decoration: few thin strands
    of pared orange rind, optional
for serving: lightly whipped
    cream, or ice cream

Crêpes suzette
POWER LEVEL: 100% (FULL) AND 70%
CONVENTIONAL HOTPLATE

*This recipe is sufficient to serve 6–8, allowing 2–3 crêpes each. Either make full
quantity and freeze half or make up half quantity and cook as indicated in point 6*

1 To make the batter: sift the flour, salt and sugar into a mixing bowl and
   make a well in the centre. Put the eggs, melted butter, brandy and orange
   rind into the centre of the flour. Whisk the eggs into the flour, gradually
   adding the milk as the mixture thickens. Cover the batter and set aside for
   at least 1 hr.
2 To make the filling: beat the butter with the sugar and orange rind until
   it is light and fluffy. Gradually beat in 1 × 15ml tbsp (1tbsp) of the orange
   juice, and the orange curaçao or grand marnier.
3 To make the pancakes: melt a little butter in a well-seasoned 15cm (6in)
   pancake pan, or frying pan. When the butter is hot, pour off the excess.
   Pour just enough batter into the pan to cover the bottom thinly (the
   pancakes should be very thin). Cook the pancake for 1 min, or until the
   underneath is lightly browned, then turn it over and cook the other side
   for 1 min. Remove the cooked pancake from the pan and set it aside.
   Make more pancakes in exactly the same way until all the batter is used
   up. You should have about 22 pancakes in all.
4 Spread each pancake with a little of the orange butter, then fold neatly
   into 4 to form a triangle.
5 Lightly butter a large, shallow, heat-resistant dish. Arrange the pancakes,
   overlapping, in the dish. Spread any remaining orange butter over the
   pancakes, then pour 3 × 15ml tbsp (3tbsp) of orange juice over the top.
   Cover the dish with clingfilm, pulling back 1 corner to vent.
6 Just before serving, cook the pancakes on 70% setting for 3½–4½ min
   (or 2½–3 min for half quantity) until they are thoroughly heated through.
   Pour the rum into a small dish and heat for 20–30 sec.
7 To serve: remove the clingfilm from the pancakes. Take the pancakes and
   the hot rum to the table, pour the rum over the pancakes and ignite
   immediately. Decorate, if liked, with a few strands of thinly pared orange
   rind and serve hot, with lightly whipped cream, or ice cream.

Salmon Trout in Aspic (page 109)

MENU FOR 8

Coquilles saint-jacques
★   ★   ★
Chicken and chicory polonaise
Pommes parisienne
★   ★   ★
Brandy-snap cups with ginger ice cream

The following timetable is a guide to the order of preparation and cooking for serving dinner at 8.30 pm, but can be easily adapted for a lunch-time meal if required.

Day before
Make the brandy-snap cups and store in an airtight tin.
Prepare and freeze the ginger ice cream.

Morning or afternoon
Prepare the potato balls for the pommes parisiennes and place in cold water until required.
Prepare the chicory heads and trim the chicken breasts.
Prepare and cook the coquilles saint-jacques ready for reheating and browning later.
Assemble all the equipment and ingredients ready for cooking from about 7.15 pm.

Order of cooking
7.15   Cook the pommes parisienne and place in a serving dish.
7.35   Cook the chicken in the browning dish and keep warm.
8.00   Cook the chicory hearts. Drain and toss in the melted butter.
       Remove the ice cream from the freezer to the refrigerator to soften, or remove when required and soften in the microwave.
8.15   Reheat the scallops in their shells and brown the tops under a hot grill. Cook the tomatoes.
8.30   Serve the first course.

While clearing away the dishes from the first course, put the main-course dishes to reheat if necessary and assemble the chicken and chicory polonaise. After the main course, soften the ice cream in the microwave if removed straight from the freezer and place a scoopful in each brandy-snap cup. Serve straight away.

for the potato purée:
675g (1½lb) potatoes, peeled
3 × 15ml tbsp (3tbsp) salted water
25g (1oz) butter
2 × 15ml tbsp (2tbsp) hot milk

for the scallops:
8–12 scallops and 8 shells (or individual shell dishes)
1 shallot, sliced
salt
6 peppercorns
½ bay leaf
150ml (¼pt) water
squeeze of lemon juice

Coquilles saint-jacques   *colour page 115*
POWER LEVEL: 100% (FULL) AND 70%

1   Cut the potatoes into even-sized pieces and cook, covered, with the salted water on 100% (full) setting for 13–15 min until tender, stirring once halfway through. Drain and purée with the butter and milk.
2   Wash the scallops and scrub the shells. Place the scallops into a bowl or dish with the shallot, salt, peppercorns, bay leaf, water and lemon juice. Cover and cook for 5 min on 70% setting.
3   Cut the tomatoes into quarters and remove the cores and seeds. Cut each quarter in half.
4   Melt the butter in a bowl for 1 min on 100% (full) setting, stir in the flour and blend well. Add the milk gradually, mixing until smooth, and add the cooking liquid from the scallops.
5   Cook for 3–4 min until thickened and boiling, stirring every minute. Stir in the tomatoes, parsley and seasoning to taste.

6   Slice or quarter the scallops and divide between the shells or shell dishes. Spoon over the sauce and pipe the potato purée round the edge. Sprinkle with the browned breadcrumbs and top with tiny slivers of butter.
7   Reheat 4 at a time for 2–3 min on 70% setting or brown the tops under a hot grill. Serve immediately.

DO NOT FREEZE

2 tomatoes, skinned
25g (1oz) butter
25g (1oz) flour
150ml (¼pt) creamy milk, approximately
1 × 5ml tsp (1tsp) finely chopped parsley
4 × 15ml tbsp (4tbsp) browned breadcrumbs
slivers butter

Chicken and chicory polonaise   *colour page 115*
POWER LEVEL: 100% (FULL)

1   Dry the chicken breasts well and beat lightly with the heel of the hand to flatten slightly. Toss in wholemeal flour which has been seasoned with salt and freshly ground black pepper.
2   Preheat a large browning dish for 6 min. Add about 40g (1½oz) of the butter and quickly add the chicken, pressing down against the hot surface of the dish with a heatproof spatula.
3   Cover and cook for 14–18 min, turning the chicken breasts over halfway through and rearranging the outside ones to the centre and vice versa. Leave on the browning dish to keep warm.
4   Place the chicory heads in a large bowl or dish with the tender leaves towards the centre of the dish and the hearts towards the outside. Sprinkle with the lemon juice, add the salted water, cover and cook for 10–12 min until tender. Drain.
5   Cut a cross on the base of each tomato and arrange in a circle with the tops down on a plate. Cover and cook for 4 min until tender.
6   Melt the rest of the butter for 1–2 min and add to the chicory. Toss over so that the heads are lightly coated in the butter.
7   Reheat the chicken if necessary for 2–3 min and arrange on a hot serving platter with some of the chicory heads and garnish with 1–2 tomatoes.
8   Mix the hard-boiled egg with the breadcrumbs and heat for 1 min. Sprinkle over the chicken and chicory and garnish with chopped parsley. Serve with the remaining chicory and tomatoes handed separately.

DO NOT FREEZE

8 chicken breasts, skinned and boned
40–50g (1½–2oz) wholemeal flour
salt and freshly ground black pepper
50–75g (2–3oz) butter
8 chicory heads, trimmed, and outer leaves removed
1 lemon, juice
6 × 15ml tbsp (6tbsp) salted water
8 tomatoes
2 hard-boiled eggs, shelled and chopped
5–6 × 15ml tbsp (5–6tbsp) toasted breadcrumbs
for garnish: chopped parsley

Pommes parisienne   *colour page 115*
POWER LEVEL: 100% (FULL)

These potato balls can be plainly boiled in the microwave or cooked in butter

1   Scoop out the potato balls with a cutter. This should produce about 900g (2lb) potato balls. Rinse well and dry.
2   Place them into a casserole dish with the salted water or melt the butter first in the dish for 1½–2 min, then add the potato balls to the dish. Toss the potatoes well in the butter.
3   Cover and cook for 15–18 min, tossing or stirring well twice throughout. Sprinkle with chopped parsley before serving.

1½kg (3lb) potatoes, peeled
6 × 15ml tbsp (6tbsp) salted water *or* 75g (3oz) butter
for garnish: chopped parsley

50g (2oz) caster sugar
50g (2oz) butter
50g (2oz) golden syrup
50g (2oz) plain flour, sifted
¼ × 5ml tsp (¼tsp) ground ginger
1 × 5ml tsp (1tsp) brandy

for the ice cream:
275ml (½pt) single cream
275ml (½pt) double cream
175g (6oz) caster sugar
175g (6oz) ginger-snap biscuits, finely crushed
4 × 15ml tbsp (4tbsp) ginger syrup
175g (6oz) preserved ginger, drained and finely chopped

for the sauce:
6 × 15ml tbsp (6tbsp) clear honey
2 × 15ml tbsp (2tbsp) brandy
4 × 15ml tbsp (4tbsp) ginger syrup
4 × 15ml tbsp (4tbsp) water
75g (3oz) stoned raisins, chopped

Brandy-snap cups with ginger ice cream   *colour opposite*
POWER LEVEL: 100% (FULL) AND 50%
CONVENTIONAL OVEN TEMPERATURE: 190°C (375°F) MARK 5

1   Melt the sugar, butter and golden syrup in a small bowl for 3–4 min on 100% (full) setting. Stir well to blend and then add the flour, ginger and brandy.
2   Place teaspoons of the mixture onto 2 greased baking trays, spacing the mixture well apart to allow room for it to spread. Bake in a preheated oven for 5–7 min until golden brown.
3   Leave to cool slightly then quickly lift each one from the baking tray and drape over upturned cups or oranges to shape. Allow to cool. When cold they may be stored in an airtight tin.
4   For the ice cream: whip the creams and sugar together until thick. Turn into metal freezer trays, cover with aluminium foil and place in the freezer for about 1–2 hr to harden.
5   Turn the mixture into a chilled bowl and beat well. Mix in the crushed biscuits, ginger syrup and preserved ginger. Cover and freeze for another hour. Beat well again, then freeze finally for 2 hr.
6   For the sauce: place all the ingredients into a small bowl and bring to the boil in the microwave on 100% (full) setting, then reduce to 50% and simmer for 5 min, uncovered.
7   Place the ice cream in the refrigerator 1 hr before required to allow to soften, or microwave for 20–30 sec just before serving. Place scoopfuls of the ice cream into the brandy-snap cups and serve with the sauce handed separately.

Brandy Snap Cups with Ginger Ice Cream (above); Chicken and Chicory Polonaise (page 113); Coquilles Saint-Jaques (page 112)

MENU FOR 6

Soufflés à la suisse

★   ★   ★

Braised stuffed leg of lamb
New potatoes in their jackets
Carrots flamande

★   ★   ★

Plum compôte and rich almond cake

The following timetable is a guide to the order of preparation and cooking for serving dinner at 8.30 pm, but can be easily adapted for a lunch-time meal if required.

Day before
Make the stock for the lamb and store in the refrigerator.
Prepare and complete the plum compôte and keep in a cool place.

Morning or afternoon
Make the rich almond cake.
Prepare, trim and precook the vegetables for the lamb.
Scrub the new potatoes and carrots and place in dishes ready for cooking.
Prepare the ham stuffing and fill the boned lamb. Tie ready for cooking.
Assemble all the ingredients and equipment ready for cooking from about 7 pm.

Order of cooking
7.00   Place the lamb on the precooked vegetables. Boil the stock and add to the dish with the other ingredients. Cook in the microwave.
7.50   Preheat the conventional oven to 180°C (350°F) mark 4. When the lamb is cooked, place the joint in the oven to brown. Place the braising vegetables on a serving platter or dish. Make the gravy and place in a serving jug.
8.00   Prepare and cook the soufflés in the microwave. At the final stage, place in the preheated oven for 15 min to brown.
8.15   Cook the carrots and leave to stand. Place the potatoes in the microwave to cook.
8.30   Serve the first course.

When clearing the first course and dishing up the main course, reheat the braising vegetables, carrots, potatoes and gravy. Carve the meat at the table.

40g (1½oz) butter
40g (1½oz) flour
225ml (8fl oz) milk
salt and freshly ground black
    pepper
½ × 5ml tsp (½tsp) nutmeg
75g (3oz) parmesan cheese
3 egg yolks
2 egg whites
275ml (½pt) double cream

Soufflés à la suisse
POWER LEVEL: 100% (FULL) AND 70%
CONVENTIONAL OVEN TEMPERATURE: 180°C (350°F) MARK 4

1   Melt the butter in a bowl for 1–1½ min on 100% (full) setting. Stir in the flour and blend well together. Add the milk gradually, mixing thoroughly after each addition.
2   Cook for 3–4 min, whisking every 30 sec until thickened and boiling. Season to taste with salt, pepper and the nutmeg.
3   Beat in half the parmesan cheese and the 3 egg yolks. Whisk the egg whites and fold into the sauce until evenly distributed.
4   Divide the mixture between 6 lightly buttered individual ramekin dishes. The mixture should fill the dishes no more than two-thirds full.
5   Arrange the ramekins in a circle on the microwave cooker shelf and cook for 4–5 min on 70% setting until slightly risen and firm. Turn or rearrange the dishes halfway through if necessary.

6 Lightly butter a large gratin dish and sprinkle with a little of the remaining parmesan cheese. Ease the soufflés out of their dishes and invert them onto the gratin dish, spacing them out slightly.

7 Pour over the cream and sprinkle with the remaining cheese. Bake in a preheated oven for 15–20 min until glazed and lightly brown in colour, or brown the tops slowly under a medium-hot grill. Serve straight away.

DO NOT FREEZE

Braised stuffed leg of lamb
POWER LEVEL: 100% (FULL) AND 50%

1 Drain the anchovies. Lay the slices of ham or gammon on a board or surface with each slice slightly overlapping. Place the anchovies on the ham, sprinkle half the chopped shallots and the herbs over and roll up into a sausage shape.

2 Place the gammon roll in the boned lamb and tie the leg securely. Weigh the prepared joint.

3 Place the onions, carrots and celery in a large casserole, cover and cook on 100% (full) setting for 6–8 min, stirring once during cooking.

4 Arrange the lamb joint on top of the vegetables and crush the garlic over the meat. Add the wine, boiling stock and bouquet garni.

5 Cover the dish and cook on 50% setting, allowing 18–20 min per 450g (1lb) stuffed lamb.

6 To make the sauce: melt the butter in a bowl or jug on 100% (full) setting for 1 min, add the remaining shallots, cover and cook for 2 min, add the flour and stir well.

7 Remove the lamb onto a chopping board, and using a draining spoon transfer the vegetables from the stock onto a serving plate. Discard the bouquet garni.

8 Use 425ml (3/4pt) of the remaining stock and add it gradually to the roux in the bowl or jug. Add the tomato purée and cook for 4–5 min, stirring every minute until thickened.

9 While the sauce is cooking, either slice the lamb or brown the joint in a hot oven or under a preheated grill to carve later at the table. Place the lamb slices or the joint on the bed of vegetables.

10 Season the sauce to taste with salt and freshly ground black pepper and serve either poured over the sliced meat or as an accompaniment to the joint to be carved.

1 × 50g (2oz) can anchovy fillets, drained and soaked in milk
225g (8oz) lean slices ham or gammon
2 shallots, finely chopped
1 × 5ml tsp (1tsp) chopped fresh parsley
1 × 5ml tsp (1tsp) chopped mixed fresh marjoram and thyme
1½kg (3lb) leg lamb, boned
2 onions, chopped
2 carrots, diced
2 sticks celery, chopped
2 cloves garlic, crushed
150ml (1/4pt) red wine
275ml (1/2pt) boiling brown stock (page 20)
bouquet garni
25g (1oz) butter
1 × 15ml tbsp (1tbsp) flour
1 × 15ml tbsp (1tbsp) tomato purée
salt and freshly ground black pepper

Carrots flamande
POWER LEVEL: 100% (FULL)

1 Leave the carrots whole if small, otherwise cut them in halves or quarters lengthwise. Place them in a bowl or dish with the salted water, butter and sugar.

2 Cover the dish with a lid or clingfilm and cook for 8–10 min until the carrots are tender, stirring once or twice throughout the cooking time.

3 Add the peas, mint and freshly ground black pepper to the dish and mix well together. Cover and cook for a further 6–7 min. Remove the lid or clingfilm and continue to cook until the water has evaporated, about 2–3 min.

4 Remove the sprig of mint, adjust the seasoning to taste and serve hot.

450g (1lb) new carrots, washed and scrubbed
3 × 15ml tbsp (3tbsp) salted water
25g (1oz) butter
2 × 5ml tsp (2tsp) caster sugar
450g (1lb) frozen peas
sprig mint
freshly ground black pepper

675g (1½lb) dessert plums
100–175g (4–6oz) caster sugar
275ml (½pt) boiling water
275ml (½pt) port or red wine
1 orange, grated rind
sugar to taste
25g (1oz) flaked almonds
for serving: cream

Plum compôte
POWER LEVEL: 50% AND 100% (FULL)

1   Wash the plums and prick each one once with a fork. Sprinkle with caster sugar and cook in a covered dish on 50% setting for 8–10 min until just tender. Shake or stir gently twice throughout.
2   Mix the boiling water with the port or wine in a large bowl or jug. Stir in the orange rind and bring to the boil on 100% (full) setting.
3   Pour the water and wine over the plums and allow to stand for 10 min. Remove the plums from the wine with a slotted spoon and place in a serving dish.
4   Add extra sugar to the wine to taste. Bring back to the boil in the microwave and boil until reduced by a third. Pour over the plums.
5   Place the almonds on a heatproof plate and cook in the microwave for 5–6 min until lightly brown. Toss them over once halfway through.
6   Scatter the almonds over the top of the dish and serve warm or chilled with cream.

150g (5oz) butter
175g (6oz) caster or light brown sugar
3 eggs, beaten
100g (4oz) ground almonds
50g (2oz) plain flour
few drops almond essence
caster or icing sugar for dusting

Rich almond cake
POWER LEVEL: 70%

1   Lightly grease a 17·5cm (7in) microwave cake dish and line the base with a circle of greaseproof paper or baking parchment.
2   Cream the butter, add the sugar and beat well together until light and fluffy. Add the eggs gradually, beating well after each addition.
3   Fold in the almonds, flour and almond essence with a metal spoon and turn the mixture into the prepared container.
4   Cook for 6–7 min until slightly moist on the top, turning the dish if necessary once halfway through.
5   Leave to stand for 10–15 min before turning onto a wire rack to cool. Serve dusted with caster or icing sugar.

Index

Other microwave books by Val Collins

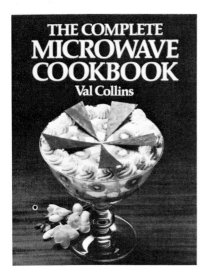

At last, in one handsome book, everything you need to know about microwave cookery—from a simple explanation of cooking techniques to a superb selection of recipes. Extensive information, delicious recipes, full colour photographs and delightful line drawings make it the one book every microwave cook will need. The recipes are to suit every taste, with detailed explanation of the methods to ensure the most delicious results.

Here is an ideal paperback that will give you all the background information you will need to become a microwave expert.

Val Collins explains in simple terms what microwave energy is and how it works. It is packed with ideas and appetising recipes too!

Probably more than any other food, fish benefits from being cooked by microwave as the moist texture and delicate flavour is preserved.

Val Collins provides a wealth of information and delicious recipes for a wide range of dishes: soups and starters; main courses such as haddock with orange and walnut stuffing and exotic dishes such as squid with mushrooms or scampi à la crème.

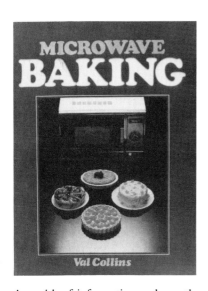

A wealth of information and mouthwatering recipes for the complete range of baking needs. Instructions are included for using conventional baking methods and combinations of microwave and conventional oven use.

Treat your family and friends to the real flavour of fruits and vegetables, cooked to perfection, looking and tasting better than those cooked by any other method. Details on freezing, blanching and drying herbs.

Wholefoods and the microwave are a perfect partnership for healthy eating. From the collection of recipes you can prepare delicious and nutritious meals – try barley pot and delightful summer sunset trifle.